*How God
Deals with Evil*

Biblical Perspectives on Current Issues

HOWARD CLARK KEE, General Editor

How God Deals with Evil

W. SIBLEY TOWNER

THE WESTMINSTER PRESS
PHILADELPHIA

Scripture quotations from the Revised Standard
Version of the Bible are copyright, 1946 and 1952,
by the Division of Christian Education of the
National Council of Churches,
and are used by permission.

BOOK DESIGN BY DOROTHY E. JONES

Published by The Westminster Press ®
Philadelphia, Pennsylvania

Printed in the United States of America

Library of Congress Cataloging in Publication Data

Towner, Wayne Sibley.
    How God deals with evil.

    (Biblical perspectives on current issues)
    Bibliography: p.
    Includes index.
    1. Judgment of God. 2. Redemption.
3. Theodicy. I. Title. II. Series.
BT180.J8T68   231'.8   76–24916
ISBN 0–664–24127–1

Some say that . . . to the gods we are like the flies that the boys kill on a summer day, and some say, on the contrary, that the very sparrows do not lose a feather that has not been brushed away by the finger of God.

Thornton Wilder
The Bridge of San Louis Rey

CONTENTS

FOREWORD

When tragedy strikes, the victim often asks, "What have I done to deserve this?" Or, "Why did God do this to me?" When someone commits a ghastly crime, the reaction is often, "I hope he gets what is coming to him!" The problem underlying such questions and comments is not trivial, although the formulations may be trite. At stake is the issue of justice in God's ordering of his creation. How does God deal with evil? This question is as current as today's news and as old as mankind. One understanding of how God deals with evil is what theologians call divine retribution.

Item

"But a man named Ananias with his wife Sapphira sold a piece of property, and with his wife's knowledge he kept back some of the proceeds, and brought only a part and laid it at the apostles' feet. But Peter said, 'Ananias, why has Satan filled your heart to lie to the Holy Spirit and to keep back part of the proceeds of the land? While it remained unsold, did it not remain your own? And after it was sold, was it not at your disposal? How is it that you have contrived this deed in your heart? You have not lied to men but to God.' When Ananias heard these words, he fell down and died. And great fear came upon all who heard of it." (Acts 5:1–5.)

That is divine retribution as understood in the early church. And that is a problem, isn't it!

Item

"Mary H——, of B—— C——, in Hampshire, who was living in service at Winchester, was curling her hair, and could not adjust it exactly as she wished. For this slight cause she uttered the horrid blasphemy of saying, 'D——the hair, and those that made it.' She instantly fell down *dead!!!!* TAKE HEED." (From *The Christian Guardian,* Vol. VI [1814], p. 169; cited in G. Rowell, *Hell and the Victorians* [Oxford University Press, 1974], pp. 1–2.) That is divine retribution as understood in the Victorian era. And that is stupid, isn't it! But the problem remains.

Item

"Lay preacher Gert Yssel, chairman of South Africa's anti-mini league, has prophesied doom and divine wrath ever since local girls hoisted their hemlines. . . . [When] western Cape Province was rocked by an earthquake which killed nine people and caused millions of dollars damage . . . Yssel immediately issued a statement blaming miniskirts for the disaster." (AP dispatch from Pretoria, South Africa, dated Feb. 4, 1970.)

That is divine retribution as understood in the twentieth century. And that is ridiculous, isn't it! But the problem remains.

Why shouldn't we solve the problem by simply rejecting the entire notion of divine retribution? We could then get away from these silly attempts to link the whole gamut of human disasters to some punitive activity of God. Unfortunately, the solution is not that simple. It may be relatively easy to move beyond the level of naiveté reflected in these quotations. But few of us will altogether give up the idea that God somehow punishes the big evildoers—the Hitlers and the Mansons and the Judas Iscariots of this world—and rewards the saints. In fact, the fear that God will punish our wrongdoing and the hope that he will punish the sins of our enemies are among our most elemental religious impulses.

These impulses have their analogies in the secular sphere as well. Public life seems to be shifting toward a more rigorous interpretation of criminal law and more vigorous use of those sanctions which are human equivalents of the penalties of divine retaliation. Surely most of us were right with Senator Ervin in the secular setting of the Watergate hearings when he used the Biblical adjuration, "Be not deceived; God is not mocked: for whatsoever a man soweth, that shall he also reap" (Gal. 6:7 KJV). Surely a governor speaks for many when he says with a smile, as he signs a bill restoring the death penalty in his state, "Now I hope we'll see a few executions around here!"

Finally, the Bible itself gives us no warrant simply to throw away the notion of God as judge and retributor. The motif of divine retribution is a powerful one in all parts of both the Old and New Testaments. It is one of the important themes by which the canonical writers sought to depict God's way of dealing with human autonomy and sin. Although it stands in relationship with—and is even subordinate to—other Biblical themes, it has to be reckoned with seriously.

Problems concerning divine retribution constantly confront lay and professional ministries within the religious communities. These problems will continue as long as people interpret events as divine rewards or punishments, or continue to blame God for doing things to them, or fear divine reprisal for expressing their own anger. As long as people continue to worry over the fate of those who have not warded off God's retributive wrath by making one Christian confession or another, the issue remains.

Because the motif is so current, and so much of the imagery of God as judge and retributor is Biblical in origin, I have undertaken to write this book to demonstrate the practical implications of Biblical theology. Using a method described in the first chapter, I have explored the entire sweep of the canon to show the range and complexity of Biblical thought on the matter of divine retribution, and the way it is inextricably bound up with its obverse counterpart, the Biblical motif of the divine will to redeem the creation. In the process, I have attempted to illustrate a method for dealing with a subject that pervades the whole Bible which is neither confined to one chronological or literary stratum of it nor always identified with a particular set of key words. As an exercise in Biblical theology, my studies attempt to assemble and organize the Biblical data that cluster around the theme without ever reducing all of them into a single, consistent, and synthetic "Biblical doctrine of retribution." The Bible contains no such doctrine—only a profoundly important motif intertwined with others.

At the beginning of a study such as this, it is well to reveal one's *a priori* commitments. Mine include these three: First of all, common sense and daily experience have convinced me that the day-to-day events of my life and the lives of others are essentially secular in origin and reality. Although everything takes place within a world upheld by God's providential care, the accidents, successes, tragedies, and satisfactions of life result from the impingement of physical and social factors upon us and not from any direct intervention by God. Included in this vast and sober reality are even the greatest events of our lives, our own births and deaths. Second, I bring to this study the prior conviction that God is Immanuel. He moves with us, he is near to us, through all our days, giving us the perceptions necessary to cope with events and make them meaningful. He even gives us the courage to alter the course of events more nearly in the direction of his Kingdom. Third, I am convinced by logic and deep intuition, as well as by my reading of the Scriptural record, that God's purpose in the world is to save it, all of it, from utter defacement and ultimate destruction and to preserve it, all of it, to be his joy and companion forever. All the proximate cause-and-effect sequences, all the historical joys and tragedies, all the retributions, great and small, are framed by his ultimate power to complete that purpose to redeem the world for himself.

In the chapters that follow, I seek to be a responsible exegete and interpreter, letting the truth emerge from the Scripture where it will, no matter what these *a priori* convictions of mine may dictate. Against the language of the Bible my first conviction will sound a dissonant note; the second should ring true. The third receives strong support and confirmation, I hope to show, not so much by individual texts and key words but by the very architecture and framework of the Bible itself.

My thanks are due to a number of people who have helped shape my thought, identified my errors, and encouraged me to continue. The editor of this series, Howard Clark Kee, has given me valued and timely communications. Kenneth Hindman, pastor of Westminster Presbyterian Church, Dubuque, Iowa, helped me give form to this project in its initial stages. More recently, I have gained much from discussions of the issues of this book with Mathias Rissi, my neighbor, colleague, and friend at·Union Theological Seminary in Virginia. Persons studying at the seminary who joined me in working through much of the material include Paul Alverson, Jr., Neil Bain, Ted Fuson, W. D. Hasty, Jr., Gordon Huffaker, Rena Lewis, John Monroe, Samuel "Skip" Murdock, and Donald Retzer. For the theses and conclusions that follow they bear no responsibility; for the author's gratitude they do. To Carolyn Messimer I express my appreciation for expert help in the preparation of the manuscript. Finally, I wish to thank Jane Miller Towner, my wife, for her willing co-reflection on the searching religious issues which this study raises. We have grown in perception together—a true reward indeed!

W. S. T.

Chapter I

THE PASTORAL PROBLEM
OF PUNISHMENT

Because this book is an exercise in practical Biblical theology, perhaps the best way to begin it is to tell four little stories. These vignettes are drawn from the vast range of human problems both outward and inward that confront anyone who seeks to minister in Christ's name. Furthermore, these incidents all turn in one direction or another around the question of punishment, human or divine, now or in the future.

The Father and the Problem Child. James dropped out of school and refused to go back. He was heavily into the drug subculture, spending most of his nights out of the house with a group of friends, many of whom obviously needed psychiatric care. He told his father that these friends were the most meaningful people he had known in his life. Yet, it seemed clear to the father that they were contributing substantially to the increasing inability of James to cope with the normal expectations of school and society.

One day James "totaled" the family car against a utility pole a few blocks from the house and shortly afterward threw down the keys on the kitchen table in a gesture of defiance. The next day his father and mother for the first time visited a family counselor at the county mental health center. The counselor challenged both parents to say what they really felt about their son's participation in the drug scene and his behavior generally. The ensuing conversation was polite until in the middle of it the counselor suddenly shouted: "You people drive me crazy. I know you are deeply angered by your son but you won't face it. You won't admit that you hate his guts! You won't admit that what he is doing is wrong and that you hate it and that it runs against every bit of your grain. You won't let him see that, either."

That evening James sauntered into the house an hour late for supper, smelling of pot and prepared to put down anybody who stood in his way. Suddenly his father slammed his fist on the supper table with a force that surprised everyone and said to the boy, "Your cocky behavior makes me sick to death!" With that he gave him a box across the ears that sent the boy flying backward out of his chair and knocked two plates off the table. The boy rose with a look of hatred on his face and said, "You can hit me all you want but I'm not going to conform to your life-style." Thereupon the father chased James around the house and on several occasions angrily laid hands upon him.

In the aftermath of this outbreak the father wept with his wife and asked repeatedly: "How can I make amends for this outburst? It just isn't Christian to act like this!"

The Uptight College Girl. The president and the dean of the seminary were relaxing in an outdoor café in "underground Atlanta" during a break in the annual meeting of the theological committee of the denomination. Their conversation ranged freely over a number of topics, then centered on the subject of language instruction in seminary. After about ten minutes of discussion of Hebrew and Greek, the president noticed that a very attractive and mod-looking college girl at the next table seemed to be paying very close attention to the conversation. He drew her in by asking, "Are you interested in Greek and Hebrew?" The girl replied, "Yes. I am thinking of spending some time on a kibbutz in Israel during the coming year." "What draws you to Israel?" asked the dean. "I want to be there because I believe that is where it is going to happen."

"What is going to happen?" asked the president.

"Christ is going to return to earth to meet his true believers," said the girl.

This surprising opening led quickly into a discussion of the convictions of the girl that the world was entering its endtime and that the premillennial rapture was near at hand. Much to the amazement of the dean and president, the girl poured forth a torrent of impassioned comment and pleading. "I hope you men are Christians. God will not spare those who have had the opportunity to confess Jesus Christ but have refused to do so with all their heart. On the day of rapture, only those who have confessed Jesus will be taken and all the rest will be left. My own parents will be left. Oh, they are nominal Christians. They raised me in the Episcopal Church. I went to church and was confirmed as a child, but in high school and college I gave up religion and experimented with drugs and sex and many different ideas. But since my conversion two years ago I have seen how foolish and shallow my parents' religion is, as was my own before. Now I know the truth that God has a purpose for those who with all their hearts have confessed him, and that purpose is to bring them out of this world of sin and evil. Can't you see all around you evidence of this sin? Can't you see how communism is sweeping the world and how it is now dominating the Congress of the United States and the White House? The United States cannot survive the coming fire. That is why I want to go to Israel. There every valley will be exalted and every mountain will be made a plain. I know you men are theological teachers, probably in a liberal seminary. I implore you, harden not your hearts, for we are near the day of judgment."

About this time the girl's mother appeared. She told her that she was closing the shop of which she was the proprietor and had to hurry home, and forcibly took the girl's arm and removed her from the scene. The girl, obviously agitated, left with a mother who seemed upset by the rhetoric she sensed must have been filling the air.

God Gave Me a Disease. By the time Lucy arrived at the door of her pastor's study, she was already a deeply confused and troubled girl. Always active in the church youth group and participating in church activities with her parents, Lucy was also a pretty and popular girl. She found a certain amount of sexual activity to be a desirable and necessary part of life for her. Although she had considerable guilt feelings about this, she felt driven by an irresistible urge to experiment further. And now, just the day before, she had learned from a private visit to an outpatient clinic in the city that she had indeed contracted gonorrhea.

Now she was in the quiet of her pastor's study, begging him not to reveal her secret to her parents. "I deserve this disease! I deserve this! I should be punished! This gonorrhea is a punishment from God for my playing around. I've talked to only one other person, my friend Shirley, and she agrees with me. I know why God is doing this to me. It's not only because I have sex with Phil, but because I want to keep on having it. I don't really want to quit or break off the relationship and yet now I will have to so that he does not get the disease, too. I don't know how I got it. It must have been one of those occasions when we were on the trip with the band.

"Mr. Blackwood, will God take the disease from me if I promise to stop having sexual relations with Phil? I knew this was going to happen! I knew it was too good to last!"

A week later Mrs. Smith, Lucy's mother, was in the pastor's study in tears. She had learned indirectly about her daughter's problem from a friend who worked in the lab at the clinic. "Why is God doing this to us?" she was asking. "Lucy and all the rest of our family have always been good church people. Why is this happening now? Can't you give us some answer?"

On What Basis Mission? Sam Slaytor was a highly effective and respected missionary in a Lebanese secondary school related to the Presbyterian Church. He was finding himself daily more deeply entangled in the mesh of vocational and religious uncertainty that threatened to swallow him up. All around him, at the Beirut University College and at the American University of Beirut, his former students had developed into attractive, sophisticated, and totally secular people. Their teachers, his colleagues on the faculties of these schools, were people of high moral and religious character, often far better educated and indeed far more perceptive than Sam felt himself to be. Among these only very few professed any kind of Christian faith. Some were practicing Muslims, some were of Eastern Orthodox or Eastern rite Catholic churches, but the vast majority were simply secular people. Most were good, earnest, and usually responsible people. Sometimes their lives were tragic, sometimes joyous; but in this respect they seemed no different from the Christians whom Sam had known back in America or indeed his fellow fraternal workers and the Protestant clergymen in the Evangelical Church in Lebanon.

Many questions had begun to press Sam more severely day by day. What would these people gain by embracing the Christian faith? The lives of many, of course, could be enriched by a vital faith of some kind. On the other hand, many others seemed to feel fulfilled and indeed very happy in the faith they had or in their secular agnosticism. What form would the preaching of the gospel among such people take? Above all, what was God's ultimate purpose for such people? Sam was haunted as always by the words of John 14:6, words that had contributed to his missionary calling in the first place, "no one comes to the Father, but by me." Yet, of one thing Sam had grown more certain year after year: the threat of everlasting punishment for all those who do not make a formal profession of faith in Jesus Christ as their personal Savior seemed totally irrelevant to these people. Somehow,

Sam had come to feel, Christ loves them too, just as they are. Still, Sam was not certain how that assurance, that deep conviction of his, measured up to the standards of the New Testament. He felt sure it would not agree with the standards of the church people back home who had sent him to be their missionary.

The father, the uptight college girl, Lucy, and Sam each have their private problems; however, they have in common with each other and with most of us a cluster of religious questions as well. The questions in this cluster have to do with God, God's wrath, God's wrathful response to human sin and folly here and now, and God's wrathful response to human sin at the end of time on a day of judgment. The religious questions which infuse and confuse the thinking of all these people have their origins in the Bible and are often couched in Biblical language. Clusters of religious questions like these lie at the heart of the pastoral problems which arise from the Biblical motif[1] of divine retribution, which motif is the subject of this study.

"Retribution," derived from the Latin verb *retribuere*, "to give back," means "requital according to merits or deserts—especially for evil."[2] In religious thought the term commonly applies to God's action in rewarding those who obey him or, more frequently, punishing those who disobey him. The problem for each of the principal characters in the four vignettes above is that the time-honored Biblical affirmation that God rewards those who obey him and punishes those who disobey his law no longer provides an adequate framework in which to interpret experience. All the characters in these vignettes, like all the rest of us who live in the latter part of the twentieth century, are experiencing a rapidly changing public environment. The tenets of civil, moral, and criminal law are being reexamined. The value of retribution as a powerful deterrent to antisocial behavior has long been giving ground in the public mind to a view of punishment that stresses the possibility of "rescuing" human beings through professional correctional care. All of us live in a religious environment in which the theme of God as the angry and retributive judge has been left for a few reactionary sectarians to develop into cartoon books to be handed out in bus stations.

Yet, for the characters of these four pastoral vignettes and for the rest of us as well, the reality of evil in the world and imperfection in the self is felt more strongly than ever. Our friends seek assurance that the evil and unfaith around them and within them will be defeated and goodness somehow vindicated. At the same time they are increasingly insecure with the religious formulae that in former years gave this assurance. One of the characters, the uptight college girl, has sought in recrudescent fundamentalism release from the confusion of living in the midst of evil without an adequate set of working moral and religious principles. For her, the necessary assurance is now provided through Biblically literalistic affirmations of judgment, hell, world catastrophe, and tribulation. The missionary teacher, on the other hand, continues to live in the midst of the uncertainty created in his mind by his own rejection of the familiar Biblical affirmation that salvation is possible only through faith in Christ. The father of the problem child, incapable of overcoming his own permissiveness with the force of righteous anger because he confused the latter with repression and destructive hostility, created a welter of confusion around himself. In his effort to be up to date about the matter of reward-and-punishment, he fell into the trap of refusing to indicate to his son what was right and what was wrong.

Although the vignettes do not all say so specifically, one may assume that all their principal characters hope and expect that the teaching of the church would throw contemporary light upon the questions of reward, punishment, divine retribution, and future hope. I believe their expectation is legitimate. In a time in which the simple formulae of our

Biblical forefathers for determining what is pleasing and dis-
pleasing to God seems to be breaking down, all of us seek
guidance. Most of us want help, Biblical and otherwise, to
enable us see the way between the extremes of permissiveness on the one hand and punitive retribution on the other,
whether the issue be our own personal behavior or our understanding of the way in which God deals with his creation.

This book intends to speak in an appropriate and modest
way to that legitimate expectation. The task is an important
one, because the demise of the older Biblical and theological
orthodoxy on the subject of God's rewarding and punishing
activity has left a vacuum in many lives of faith. Biblical
theology can perform a service of signal contemporary importance. It can reassemble the data bearing on the motif of
divine retribution in order to sketch out a perspective on
God's justice and love which will adequately take into account all sides of the Biblical witness to the theme. In this
book, I hope to outline a Biblical approach to the question of
how God deals with sin, unbelief, and suffering which is more
adequate than the simple conviction that sinners will be punished now and in the hereafter, that much suffering is the
punishment for sin, and that those who fail to confess faith
in Jesus Christ must endure everlasting punishment.

At the same time, I shall seek to speak to these questions
in a way that is faithful to the full dimensions of the Biblical
witness, and therefore more realistic than some earlier attempts by liberal theology to dismiss the problem of evil. The
Bible makes graphic the deadly seriousness of the problem
of evil. It shows that in the struggle against evil God and man
alike are caught up and scarred. Nor do I find evidence in the
Biblical witness to support a theology which would envision
an ultimate overcoming of evil by evolutionary process. The
thesis of this book is a simple one. *By its very architecture, the
Bible places the motif of divine retribution within the larger
framework of God's redemptive purpose, thereby depriving
wrath and judgment of ultimate significance.* I shall attempt

to show that the ubiquitous and profoundly significant motif of divine retribution in all of its legal, historical, prophetic, poetic, and apocalyptic expressions is juxtaposed to and finally encompassed by an equally powerful Biblical motif of human and cosmic redemption.

Both motifs are grounded in the Biblical conviction of the righteousness and compassion of the Creator; both motifs find their center point in the punished and vindicated Christ; both motifs look toward God's own triumph at the end of history. The intertwining of these two motifs in the Scripture explains why the believer finds in the Bible undoubted evidences of the motif of divine retribution when God punishes evildoers and extirpates their evil at the Eschaton; simultaneously, the believer finds God lifting up those who fall, forgiving sinners, and, through Christ's sacrifice on the cross, laying a groundwork for the redemption of the full creation. Both of these themes must be taken seriously and, without resorting to a false synthesis, their interrelationship must be shown.

This book will seek to convince those who have stressed the righteous judgment of God to the exclusion of all other aspects of his relationship to the world, and who look forward to the Eschaton as above all a refiner's fire, that they do an injustice to the nuanced character of the Biblical text. It will also seek to show those who ignore the motif of divine retribution and content themselves with saying that a nice guy like God wouldn't do bad things to his creatures that they, too, truncate the full dimension of Biblical witness.

Let the thesis of the work, however, not be misunderstood. From the broad outline of the Bible as a whole and from that all-important event at its center, evil is seen as a tragic and not a trivial matter. The acceptance by one man on a cross of the full measure of divine retribution manifests the cost of evil. At the same time his willingness to do so manifests the full measure of divine redemption. One can only conclude that the ultimate stress of Scripture must be summed up in the words, "I have no pleasure in the death of any one, says the Lord God; so turn, and live" (Ezek. 18:32).

In the pages that follow I shall attempt to support the thesis of the book. Chapter II will make a great cycle through the Bible dealing with texts that develop the motif of divine retribution. The six texts selected for special consideration are taken as representative of many others of their same literary types and horizons. In no way can the treatment of the Biblical data on the subject be exhaustive. The exegesis of the texts will illustrate the diverse expressions of the motif. It will also point out such limitations upon the applicability of the retributive role of God as the writers may imply.

Chapter III illustrates the ways in which confessional statements and other theological writings have contributed toward an unwarranted reduction of the diverse Biblical testimony into a "doctrine" of divine retribution. As a safeguard against such an error for those who wish to deal afresh with the Biblical data, I propose certain methodological principles for developing a "hermeneutic of divine retribution."

Chapter IV repeats the great cycle through the Bible begun in Chapter II. This, time, however, the track leads through the Biblical materials which incorporate and expand the great countervailing motif of divine redemption. I have tried to select for exposition six texts which match the six retributional texts of Chapter II in a number of ways. Some are drawn from similar types of literature or emanate from the same periods of Biblical history. One text of Chapter IV is even drawn from the same prophetic book as its corresponding text in Chapter II. By keeping the examples closely related in this way, I have sought to maintain a dialectic between them similar to the intense, intra-Biblical colloquy between the juxtaposed motifs of retribution and redemption.

Chapter V attempts to marshal the evidence gained from the two cycles through the Biblical text in support of the thesis of the book. It culminates in short responses to the persons introduced in the four vignettes at the beginning of this chapter. By ending the book where it began, I hope to indicate the practical impact upon human and pastoral problems of an understanding of the Biblical motif of divine retribution which sets it firmly within the larger framework of God's redemptive purpose.

Chapter II

THE DIVINE "NO"
IN THE BIBLE

The divine "no" refers to those texts within the Bible which develop the motif of divine retribution. To the evil, the unjust, and the ungodly, God speaks words of wrath and announces retaliation in the series of texts which this chapter surveys. The texts chosen range throughout the Scriptures. One text is from the Pentateuch, one each from the Prophets, wisdom materials, and apocalyptic literature of the Old Testament; one from the Gospels and one from the book of Revelation. The same pattern will be followed in dealing with each text: (1) The Revised Standard Version of the text is given. (2) I give a brief exegesis of the passage and review the scholarly literature concerning it under the heading "Discussion." (3) Finally, by means of some paragraphs on "Direction," I will attempt to show the relationship of the passage to the developing outline of the motif of divine retribution. I will also point out any limitations within the text upon an overly extended or rigid application of the general notion of divine retribution.

THE LAW OF RETALIATION

Text

22 When men strive together, and hurt a woman with child, so that there is a miscarriage, and yet no harm follows, the one

who hurt her shall be fined, according as the woman's husband shall lay upon him; and he shall pay as the judges determine. 23 If any harm follows, then you shall give life for life, 24 eye for eye, tooth for tooth, hand for hand, foot for foot, 25 burn for burn, wound for wound, stripe for stripe.

—*Exodus 21:22–25*

Discussion

This setting for the ancient *lex talionis,* "law of retaliation," itself contained in vs. 23b–25, is generally regarded as the earliest in the Old Testament. Similar statements of the law in different legal contexts are to be found in Lev. 24: 19–20 and Deut. 19:21. The only other Biblical reflection of the law is found in the Sermon on the Mount, Matt. 5:38–42.[1]

It is customary to place this law of retaliation at the beginning of all discussions of the motif of divine retribution in the Bible. As I have argued elsewhere,[2] the two are not to be equated. The term "retaliation" is commonly understood (as is confirmed by the particular legal situation of this text) as an exact payment in kind for an evil deed done.[3] "Retribution," on the other hand, can refer both to good and to evil consequences or responses to deeds done. It may or may not be determined according to the simple principle of "measure for measure." Nonetheless, the rule "eye for an eye" is certainly one of the most familiar general legal principles to be laid down in Israelite tradition. It is appropriate that we begin the discussion of the broader issue of the Biblical motif of divine retribution with this narrower statement of the principle of retaliation.

The law of retaliation, like other Israelite law, is placed at Sinai. The "Book of the Covenant" in which it stands (Ex. 20:22 to 23:33), however, presupposes in many of its stipulations a settled, agrarian environment. It is therefore commonly thought among scholars that the material in these chapters, including the *lex talionis,* substantially embodies existing Canaanite law which was taken over by Israel after the settlement in the land. With the earlier Canaanite milieu still in mind, the *lex talionis* probably was intended as a legal standard for use by public justice, the "justice in the gate," and not for private or personal vengeance. The text itself suggests as much, if the reference to "the judges" (v. 22) can be validated.[4]

Within the larger context of a series of laws on injuries (21:12–32), the law of retaliation is invoked in relation to the rather complex and obscure matter of the injury of a pregnant woman during the course of an altercation between two men. It is not absolutely clear from vs. 22–23 whether the injury in question is that sustained by the pregnant woman herself, or by her fetus born maimed or dead. Whatever the case, however, "if any harm follows" beyond the miscarriage itself, the defendant is to give "life for life, eye for eye, tooth for tooth. . . ."

The evident tension between the specific case of a woman injured in the context of a fight and the sweeping general terms of the *lex talionis* itself (vs. 24–25) has led many scholars to conclude that the law is interpolated in its present context. This contention is supported by the fact that the law clearly does not apply in all its details to the situation described. For example, how likely is it that either a fetus or a woman would be "burned" or given "stripes" as the law presupposes? And why should the sweeping *lex talionis*, unconditional in character, be brought into this series of conditional cases? The only possible answer to these questions would appear to be that the law was inserted into this setting after having had a prior life of its own in other contexts. The obvious next step, then, is to look outside of this particular setting and even outside of the Bible itself for other examples.

Such a study quickly leads to highly relevant parallels in non-Israelite ancient Near Eastern literature. Laws of retaliation comparable to the Old Testament *lex talionis* are to be found in the Code of Hammurabi (who ruled in Babylon ca. 1728–1686 B.C.). Here we read, for example: "If a son has struck his father, they shall cut off his hand. If a seignior has destroyed the eye of a member of the aristocracy, they shall destroy his eye. If he has broken a(nother) seignior's bone, they shall break his bone. . . . If a seignior has knocked out a tooth of a seignior of his own rank, they shall knock out his tooth. . . . If a seignior has struck a(nother) seignior's daughter and has caused her to have a miscarriage, he shall pay ten shekels of silver for her fetus. If that woman has died, they shall put his daughter to death."[5]

An even more dramatic ancient Near Eastern parallel to the text of Ex. 21:22–25 is text 50 of the Middle Assyrian laws, dated between 1450–1250 B.C.:

> [If a man] has struck a married [woman] and caused her to lose [the fruit of her womb, the wife of the man] who [caused] the (other) married woman [to lose] the fruit of [her womb] shall be treated as [he has] treated her; [for the fruit of] her womb he pays (on the principle of) a life (for a life). But, if that woman dies, the man shall be put to death; for the fruit of her womb he pays (on the principle of) a life (for a life). Or, if that woman's husband has no son (and) his wife has been struck and has cast the fruit of her womb, for the fruit of her womb the striker shall be put to death. If the fruit of the womb is a girl, he nonetheless pays (on the principle of) a life (for a life).[6]

Modern scholars of ancient Near Eastern law have argued that the presence of the *lex talionis* in Babylonian law, far from being a remnant of a primitive legal mentality, actually represents an advance in two ways: it eliminates class preference, for the law could be no respecter of persons; and, it prevents unbridled and excessive revenge. If one compares the Assyrian and Babylonian laws of injuries with the ancient Hittite codes, for example, one discovers in the latter that no murder or injury is considered important enough to exact from the murderer or the injurer life or any other penalty of

personal injury. It was sufficient simply to pay a cash compensation to the injured person. The cash settlement also varied
remarkably according to the relative position in society of
the two parties to the dispute. For example, a defendant
owed a lower-class individual considerably less for an injury
than the amount which could be claimed by a rich man.
Whether or not one agrees that provision of a *lex talionis*
represents an advance over this position, it is possible to
argue that the trajectory upon which this law is moving is
toward a more equitable treatment of individuals. It is interesting that, except for slaves, the *lex talionis* in Israel appears
to apply to all free men and women. This is perhaps the most
egalitarian application of the principle in all of the ancient
Near East.

One other insight can be drawn from comparisons between the law of retaliation as expressed in Ex. 21:22–25 and
the way in which other cultures deal with the problems for
which retaliation seems appropriate. Many of us commonly
assume that the idea of "eye for an eye" is so deeply rooted
in the human psyche that it is almost a universal instinct. We
point to the fact that small children make decisions in the
interpersonal sphere based upon this principle. Indeed,
there can be no doubt that the slogan is almost an intrinsic
part of the Judeo-Christian-Islamic culture of the West,
reaching its most extensive articulation and application in
Muslim countries.[7] A study of other cultures, however, suggests that even our small children have learned their *lex
talionis* from their elders and others who share our common
culture. For example, in early Navaho traditions, the penal
code was strikingly lenient in the cases which we would
consider appropriate for retaliation and retribution. For
murder there was only a cash fine; for injuries of other sorts
there were relatively minor penalties. This can be partially
explained as the outgrowth of a casual view of death and of
the low value of human life in the early Navaho culture. Yet
in another area one finds fierce threats of severe penalties.

That area is the violation of ritual taboos, and the penalties are decay and death. No individual in society was charged with the responsibility of enforcing these penalties for the violation of taboos. It was left up to the Great Spirit, in his own somewhat vague and magical way, to enforce the sanctions.[8] Although comparison with one totally separate primitive culture is slim evidence indeed, the results do support the argument that the formula "eye for an eye" is not the universal phenomenon that some have believed it to be. The law of retaliation seems primarily to be a part of our Western culture, and though it was introduced at an early date it may not be such a primitive legal form at that.

In looking at the Bible's own reflection upon the law of retaliation, one quickly discovers that the law is almost never invoked by people against other people. Even though the law appears early in the Book of the Covenant, the rest of the canon seems to be eager to back away from it. Excluding the standard death penalty for murder and other heinous offenses, and looking only at nonfatal bodily injuries for which an offender receives a like injury, one can find only one case in the entire Bible in which the law is applied by one man against another, namely, Judg. 1:7.[9] In fact, the principle proves to be preserved primarily for describing God's way of dealing with people. The prophet Isaiah puts it simply: "Woe to the wicked! It shall be ill with him, for what his hands have done shall be done to him" (Isa. 3:11).[10] The reader of the Old Testament is finally left with the impression that ultimately only God has the authority to enforce his will with decrees as terrible as those required by the *lex talionis*. Far from being the most ancient law in the Old Testament, one can suggest on the basis of this evidence that it is not even deeply rooted in the Old Testament as a principle of civil law. Whatever its *origin* may have been, its *use* in the Bible, especially to describe God's activity, may grow out of a later stage in thinking about the matter of justice. Perhaps that stage reflects the preaching of the prophets!

The process of attempting to refine and restrict the application of *lex talionis* continues in post–Old Testament times. In Matt. 5:38–42, Jesus radically reinterprets the law under the rubric "you have heard that it was said . . . but I say to you." By teaching that the gospel requires not simply tit for tat but an aggressive nonresistance to evil which offers an offender the other cheek, the cloak, and the second mile, Jesus disarms the law of retaliation. Now the law is turned around to become an opportunity whereby an injured party can bring the injurer to repentance and new life. In the context of Matt. 5:21–48—a series of teachings that reduce the ancient legal propositions to absurdity and stress the importance of the intention to do good and to redeem the evildoer—Jesus overcomes the *lex talionis* as a guide to moral behavior. Now love, not retaliation, should be a believer's response to evil.

Jewish interpretation of the law also regularly seeks to overcome it. To the Pharisaic interpreters of the Talmudic period the *lex talionis* unquestionably points to compensation and restitution rather than retribution. Like Jesus, they reduce the law to absurdity when they teach:

> R. Simon B. Yohai says: *"Eye for eye"* means pecuniary compensation. You say pecuniary compensation, but perhaps it is not so, but actual retaliation [by putting out an eye] is meant? What then will you say where a blind man put out the eye of another man, or where a cripple cut off the hand of another, or where a lame person broke the leg of another? How can I carry out in this case [the principle of retaliation] of "eye for eye," seeing that the Torah says, *Ye shall have one manner of law,* implying that the manner of law should be the same in all cases?[11]

Modern interpreters of the law of retaliation at first stressed its crassness and primitiveness. More recently, however, commentators like Martin Noth[12] and Brevard S. Childs[13] have argued that the Near Eastern background of the text and its relationship to the work of the legal assembly actually do not prove its crassness or primitiveness but rather its concern to provide judges fair guidelines for affording equal protection of law to all members of society.

A recent study of the *lex talionis* by B. S. Jackson is of particular interest.[14] Jackson shows, first of all, that the *lex talionis* itself (vs. 24–25) does not fit well with the preceding narrative situation (v. 22) and must have been interpolated. He shows that the ancient rabbinic commentators raised the question of the applicability of vs. 24–25 to the situation presupposed in v. 19, and, by such exegetical devices, tended to interpret the retaliation as a monetary reparation. Although Jackson does not believe that necessarily represents the original intention of the talion, he at least agrees that the uneasiness felt by the rabbis regarding its present setting was justified. Furthermore, he agrees with Diamond[15] in arguing that the old view which regarded "talion as being 'primitive' or 'natural,' and as representing the earliest stage of legal advance, is false."[16] One legal theory would argue that the application of a law of divine retaliation to issues of civil law is a normal evolutionary development reflecting the impact of religious theory upon law. Indeed, it is this solution for the problem of the intention of the *lex talionis* in its present context which Jackson finally adopts. He is not certain who in Israel might have inserted a concept of divine retaliation into the old legal materials found in the Book of the Covenant. His tendency would be to suggest it was the work of the Deuteronomist. This theory would also account for the presence of the formula identical with Ex. 21:24 in Deut. 19:21. Perhaps the last verse of the text, Ex. 21:25, reflects an even more highly theoretical and idealistic understanding from a later theologian such as the Priestly writer. In either case, the impact of religious theory of a somewhat idealistic and aristocratic nature seems to Jackson to be felt here. If he is right, we are dealing with a rather impractical legal principle reflecting theological interests rather than the realities of human justice as they are worked out in the course of numerous cases heard and resolved "in the gate."

Direction

In spite of the image of brutality which "an eye" in exchange for a victim's eye conjures up in the popular mind, the *lex talionis* appears to scholars to be a significant advance over earlier stages of law in Israel and the ancient Near East. The trajectory upon which it moves appears to lead toward more just civil laws. Unbridled revenge is checked and privilege is no longer a consideration in the assignment of culpability. The attempt to sketch out this trajectory, however, runs into difficulty. Throughout the history of the canon, Israel and the early Christians seem to be backing away from the *lex talionis* as a principle of civil law. The specific settings in which the law is cited seem far less significant than the categorical and universal principle itself would warrant. These citations are few and far between. In the writings of Israel's theologians and prophets, the law functions almost entirely as a way of interpreting God's dealings with his people. It is as if the sanctions suggested by the law of retaliation are too awesome for mere human justice to assign. Let God square accounts with those who violate his holy will; human law, in the meantime, will generally settle for cash!

Jackson's theory that the law represents a quintessence of legal theory introduced into the older sources by the Deuteronomists is suggestive, though impossible to prove. Taken apart from any specific case situation, the principle has a programmatic or idealistic tone. Certainly it coincides with the interests of the theologians who gave rise to the Deuteronomic interpretation of history. In that history, as we shall see in more detail, the scales of justice are nicely balanced and God deals with his erring servants in a manner that can best be described as retaliatory. Yet, whether in its formulary expression in Exodus or in its historical application in the Deuteronomic writings, the principle of retaliation as such does not seem to be in touch with a wide range of human realities. It does not reckon with the possibility of repentance and the need for pardon; it is open to human error and exploitation; the penalties which it invokes are often irrevocable. Above all, it is in principle inconsistent with the reforming and saving purpose of God so richly developed in the countervailing Biblical motif of divine redemption. Considerations such as these will be necessary if we are to place the law of retaliation in a nuanced description of the Biblical motif of divine retribution.

THE THREATENING PROPHETS

Text

1 Hear the word of the LORD, O people of Israel; for the LORD has a controversy with the inhabitants of the land. There is no faithfulness or kindness, and no knowledge of God in the land; 2 there is swearing, lying, killing, stealing, and committing adultery; they break all bounds and murder follows murder. 3 Therefore the land mourns, and all who dwell in it languish, and also the beasts of the field, and the birds of the air; and even the fish of the sea are taken away.

—*Hosea 4:1–3*

Discussion

I have chosen this short indictment-threat passage from the prophet Hosea to represent a second dimension of the Biblical motif of divine retribution. This text is representative of the prophetic judgment oracles of the classical eighth-century B.C. prophets Amos, Hosea, Micah, and I Isaiah (Isa., chs. 1 to 39).

Little needs to be said here regarding the historical situation in which Hosea and Amos, his fellow prophet of the

Kingdom of Israel, worked. The impending threat of Assyrian conquest seeps like a stain through the proclamation of judgment and doom which characterizes much of the writing of these prophets. Amos interprets the inevitable destruction of Samaria at the hands of Assyria as Yahweh's punishment of his people for having allowed political corruption and social oppression to dominate their national life. Particularly in this case of Hosea, the battle to the death between the pure religion of Yahweh and Canaan's indigenous worship of Baal adds a crucial dimension to the prophet's interpretation of history. That competition was not new in Hosea's time. Indeed, most scholars now agree that the struggle between the Baalism of the land and the Yahwistic faith of at least the core of the invaders began as soon as Israel appeared in Palestine and was not definitively settled for more than half a millennium. Only during the period of the restoration after the Babylonian exile did the Canaanite challenge finally subside. In his time, Hosea confronts that challenge with a symbolic marriage (chs. 1 to 3) and much stunning invective.

According to H.-W. Wolff,[17] Hosea was allied with Levitical circles which existed in the rural areas and towns of the Northern Kingdom during the eighth century. Biblical tradition does not give us a great deal of information about these Levitical circles. We can infer that they were disenfranchised priestly groups who taught the "old-time religion" of Yahwism, who argued the necessity of a return to the fundamentals of the Israelite faith, and who therefore represented a kind of antiestablishment learned class. Their opposition could be expected particularly in those periods when the official establishment of the royal house and priesthood engaged in detentes with the surrounding Canaanite culture and religion. Wolff[18] and other scholars also postulate a direct link between the preaching of Hosea and the Deuteronomic literature of the sixth-century B.C. Kingdom of Judah. They believe that these same Levitical circles were among those who migrated south after the fall of Samaria. It may have been from the preaching of prophetic groups such as these that the Deuteronomic and Josianic reform of 621 B.C. drew much of its impetus.

The oracle cited above is cast in the form of a "controversy" between Yahweh and his people.[19] The setting is one that would be familiar to all hearers.[20] It is a courtroom case between Yahweh and the inhabitants of the land. The prophet himself announces that the court is in session and the case is under way; the actual indictment and ensuing judgment are Yahweh's own, which the prophet merely communicates on his behalf.

The specific terms of Yahweh's indictment against Israel are found in 4:1b-2. The violation of laws against swearing, lying, killing, stealing, and committing adultery mentioned in v. 2 renders impossible the fruits of covenant obedience, faithfulness, kindness, and knowledge of God mentioned in v. 1b. Clearly the prophet assumes on the part of his hearers a general knowledge of laws prohibiting the mentioned transgressions and defining the fruits of obedience. In fact, some kind of covenant binding Yahweh, prophet, and people is presupposed. It would seem that Hosea and his hearers had knowledge of some relatively simple list of stipulations of the type preserved in the Decalogue texts of Ex. 20:1–17 and Deut. 5:6–21.

Verse 3 introduces the threat. Because of Israel's disobedience, the land "mourns" (or "shall dry up" [Mays]), the people, the beasts, and the birds "languish," and "even the fish of the sea are taken away." The prophet speaking for Yahweh appears simply to be announcing consequences of disobedience. Such an announcement need not have been received as the slashes of a flaming radical. If the simple covenant to which the prophet alludes was well known in Israel, and if it had already spelled out the consequences of disobedience as our present Decalogue does at least in part (Ex. 20:5–6; Deut. 5:9–10), then Hosea, the proclaimer of judgment, is functioning as a conservative.[21] He can be regarded as one who is trying to preserve the terms of the covenant between Yahweh and his people and who now chooses to reaffirm those terms by stressing to those who are disobedient the effect of their own disobedience.

For many years Old Testament scholars have argued that the Israelites saw themselves as a covenant people from the very beginning of their collective self-consciousness. Eichrodt, as is well known, found covenant to be a theme of the Old Testament so all-pervasive as to warrant organizing much of Old Testament theology around it.[22] It is commonly recognized that a large part of the material between Ex., ch. 20, and Num., ch. 19, was brought into the Pentateuch by later writers, including the Deuteronomists and priestly theologians of the seventh and sixth centuries B.C. Nevertheless, the fact of Sinai seems to have loomed large to prophets and historians alike from nearly the very beginning. Sinai was in some sense the constitutive moment in the nation's history. God entered into an agreement with his people which required obedience to certain laws on their part and promised reward and protection on his part. The question confronting us as we detect allusions to covenant in the preaching of the prophet Hosea is this: "How extensive was covenant ideology in the eighth century B.C., and what form did it take?"

Treaties or legal covenants between kings are known from extra-Biblical sources as early as the pre-2500 B.C. Sumerian Vulture Stele from Lagash.[23] The legal form reaches its most developed state in the Hittite suzerainty treaty documents of the late Bronze Age.[24] The fully developed treaty pattern includes the following elements: preamble; a prologue, reciting the history of the relationships between the parties; the stipulations of the covenant; provision for deposit of the text and periodic public reading; witnesses who will testify to the acquiescence of both parties in the present covenant; and, finally, curses and blessings.[25] If Israel was conscious at an early stage of this full-blown suzerainty treaty pattern for expressing covenant agreements, her literature does not reveal that consciousness. For example, the agreements reached between Yahweh and Abraham in Gen., chs. 12 to 17, must properly be described as election rather than covenant traditions. No extensive oath-supported commitment to stipulations on Abraham's part is reported. Rather, the commitments are Yahweh's own to bring out of Abraham an elect people and to carry out through Abraham his purpose. Furthermore, the Sinai tradition as we now have it does not exhibit all of the features of a reciprocal covenant or treaty. The covenant is introduced by the Decalogue and subsequently developed at the hand of the P writers to great length by the incorporation of numerous legal traditions, some old and some new. In the older strata, however, there is no mention of extensive sanctions; the section of curses and blessings which closes out the "Holiness Code" (Lev., chs. 17 to 26) probably belongs in its present form to the exilic or early postexilic period. Only in the book of Deuteronomy are Israel's covenant obligations expressed for the first time in the full-blown pattern of the suzerainty treaty, complete with sanctions of curse and blessing to be enforced by Yahweh.

An answer to the question of the extent and form of Israelite covenant ideology at the time of Hosea begins to emerge. Instead of implying a full-fledged covenant with attached sanctions of blessing and cursing, it would appear that the prophetic oracles of judgment from the eighth century B.C. were based upon a much simpler tradition of covenant obligation. In fact, prophetic preaching of judgment against transgressors of Yahweh's will may be a stage in the full development of the idea of a covenant relationship between God and his people. Before Amos and Hosea the covenant tradition may have consisted of a body of well-established case law and a smaller collection, perhaps even a decalogue, of categorical commands of Yahweh recited in cultive cove-

nant renewal occasions. A second stage in the development
of the covenant tradition would have been the prophetic
preaching itself. In the context of various threatening historical circumstances, even including destruction of Israel by her
enemies, the prophetic indictments and threats amplified
the character of the curse which falls upon those who disobey
God's will. Following the fall of Samaria in 722 B.C., the
Levitical circles and other disciples of the northern prophets
went south to Judah. There the early covenant traditions and
prophetic preaching of judgment were combined with the
prophetic tradition of the Southern Kingdom to produce the
fully developed covenant statement and attached curses-
and-blessings which constitute the book of Deuteronomy.[26]

Direction

If these suggestions are correct, the oracles of judgment
emanating from the eighth-century prophets of the Northern Kingdom, Amos and Hosea (and, for that matter, Micah
and I Isaiah in the south), point toward a development which
reaches its full fruition a century later. Only in the book of
Deuteronomy, which achieved its present form in the seventh century, does the full impact of prophetic preaching of
woe and doom to those who disobey God's commandments
receive literary expression. Couched as it is in the form of a
treaty with sanctions enforceable by God attached to it, the
relation of obedience to curses and blessing, to reward and
punishment, becomes fully explicit. In short, the book of
Deuteronomy, and not the prophetic judgment oracles, begins to emerge as the central point in the development of the
Biblical motif of divine retribution. The fierce judgment oracles of the eighth-century prophets are not that central point,
though they develop the theme of Yahweh's retributive justice to a higher degree than was ever the case in the earlier
stages of the books of Moses.

Certainly the prophetic canon knows of God's wrath toward evil and takes that wrath seriously. Yahweh will not

abide disobedience to his elemental prohibitions against lying, swearing, killing, stealing, and committing adultery. He
will extirpate these evils even if they grow up in the midst
of his own people. The prophets draw upon the full range of
the traditions of their people, written and unwritten, theological and popular, to drive home this point. Yet, the system
of reward and punishment in the prophets does not appear
to be a closed one. Their oracles of judgment do not have the
character of curses pure and simple. Underlying them, often
quite visibly, is an evangelical thrust designed to bring about
change in corrupt hearts, to win obedience, and so effect the
redemption of the nation and its individuals. It is at this point
that the retributional motif in prophetic preaching intersects
with the motif of the divine purpose to redeem the world.
Evil brings its inevitable rewards, the prophets proclaim: loss
of faithfulness, kindness, and the knowledge of God; loss of
food and raiment and homeland. But the fullness of their
message, which we shall explore further in Chapter V, knows
that the divine intention to save his people is greater even
than that people's capacity to obey God. In the last analysis,
the prophets will not push the treaty model so far that Yahweh becomes bound simply to react to the stimuli given him
by his people's disobedience or obedience. His will to redeem his people can outbalance even the massive provoca-
tion and sin which his people throw up to him.

An Ominous Cloud Over History

Text

15 See, I have set before you this day life and good, death and
evil. 16 If you obey the commandments of the LORD your God
which I command you this day, by loving the LORD your God,
by walking in his ways, and by keeping his commandments
and his statutes and his ordinances, then you shall live and
multiply, and the LORD your God will bless you in the land

which you are entering to take possession of it. 17 But if your heart turns away, and you will not hear, but are drawn away to worship other gods and serve them, 18 I declare to you this day, that you shall perish; you shall not live long in the land which you are going over the Jordan to enter and possess. 19 I call heaven and earth to witness against you this day, that I have set before you life and death, blessing and curse; therefore choose life, that you and your descendants may live, 20 loving the LORD your God, obeying his voice, and cleaving to him; for that means life to you and length of days, that you may dwell in the land which the LORD swore to your fathers, to Abraham, to Isaac, and to Jacob, to give them.

—Deuteronomy 30:15–20

Discussion

The great debates among Biblical scholars of previous generations regarding the book of Deuteronomy hardly need to be reviewed here. Let us simply assume that the book reached its present form about the time of the reform of the king Josiah (621 B.C.) and that it provided the basic orientation for the great court history preserved in I Samuel through II Kings, which was completed only late in the sixth century B.C. Although seventh-century in its present form, Deuteronomy contains many genuine ancient traditions from as early as the period of the Twelve Tribe League (Judges). Yet these traditions have all been reworded to conform with the overarching theological program of the circles which wrote the book. This program included the centralization of the Israelite cult at Jerusalem and an interpretation of history in a retributional framework which would understand all national events either as rewards for obedience or punishment for disobedience. As already indicated, some scholars identify the originators of Deuteronomy as Levitical circles from the Northern Kingdom who moved south after the destruction of Samaria in 722 B.C. Others eliminate the hypothetical Levitical element from the picture and argue

simply that the traditions of Deuteronomy are a seventh-
century culmination of the prophetic preaching of the
eighth.[27] Whoever they may have been, the Deuteronomists
set forward their program of reform with such clarity and
force that it left both a temporary mark on Israel's polity and
a permanent one on its theology.

We have already dwelt at some length upon the suzerainty
treaty pattern and its relationship to covenant-ideology in
Israel. Central to that relationship is Deuteronomy, in which
all the elements of the pattern are present, including the
powerful divine sanctions of curse and blessing. The text
before us now is the concluding paragraph of Moses' farewell
address to his people, which follows the covenant proper, the
sanctions, and provision for public reading. It is expressed in
large part in the conditional style so characteristic of the
book of Deuteronomy.

Moses opens the paragraph (v. 15) by identifying the two
options that lie before his people—life and good, death and
evil. He then informs them of the consequences of choosing
each of these directions: the choice of good will lead to life,
fruitfulness, and prosperity in the land (v. 16), but the choice
of evil will lead to exile and death (vs. 17–18). Then, to fill out
the complete outline of the treaty pattern, Moses calls
heaven and earth to be witnesses against Israel that he has
set before the people these two great choices (v. 19). His
speech concludes with an evangelical coda which exhorts the
people to choose blessing and so to inherit the good things
which God has ordained for them.

In Deuteronomy one reaches the apex of the development
of the motif of divine retribution in the Old Testament. Inasmuch as this text is quite representative of the thought of the
book on the relationship of obedience and disobedience to
divine reward and punishment, it is safe to say that the motif
of divine retribution is simple, strong, and clear in the book.
If Israel obeys, Yahweh will bless his people. If Israel dis-
obeys, an ominous cloud hangs over her history.

And yet there remains one aspect of the book in general and of this text in particular which prevents the retributional hold placed upon God and man alike from being absolutely rigid. That aspect is suggested in this text by the words "therefore choose" in v. 19b. As the English suggests, the Hebrew verb is in a form implying not-yet-completed action.[28] The choice, though urged upon the people, is not yet made. As long as that choice is not made the possibility of life for Israel and their descendants remains open.

This tiny textual feature may seem too thin a reed upon which to lean any interpretation. However, when seen in the context of the overarching literary conceit of the book of Deuteronomy—the seventh-century authors' fictional placement of Israel on the east bank of Jordan poised for entry into the Promised Land—the feature becomes significant. One might say that the choice is never made; the treaty is never signed; the curse and blessing are never activated absolutely; the option to obey remains open. In the ancient Near Eastern treaties, the parties' irrevocable decision to adhere is reported and the witnesses are sworn to that evidence. Even in Josh. 24:21ff. the people do in fact choose the Lord so that Joshua must set up stones to witness against them. In marked contrast, the witnesses here are asked simply to note that Moses has set before the people the choice. No resulting action of the people is reported. In fact, the choice to obey Yahweh's will remains as a kind of permanent option to an Israel forever poised on the east bank of the Jordan. This is an important mitigating element in an otherwise cut-and-dried retributional scheme in Deuteronomy.[29] The book makes it clear that life and death hinge upon the choice made here and now and that Yahweh will implement the curse against those who disobey his laws and his statutes. Nevertheless, history is left open at the end in the hope that the choice may yet be life.

That open-endedness continues to be felt in the Deuteronomic historical work, in spite of its frequently heavy-handed analysis of events. It continues down to the very last verse of II Kings. That verse pictures Jehoiachin, the last remaining member of the house of David, still alive and seated with the vassal kings at the table of the king of Babylon. The history of the Kingdom of Judah appears to be at an end. The curse appears to have been fully implemented, except that this one man remains seated and eating in Babylon. Precisely because he remains, the possibility of national restoration flowing from a decision to obey God remains as well. Is it possible to say that this ending opens the Deuteronomic history out onto a larger Biblical scheme of redemption wherein Yahweh's power to save his people proves greater than his obligation to implement against them the curse which their disobedience has earned?

Direction

For some decades a kind of scholarly orthodoxy has assumed that, from Mosaic times onward, Israel was heavily influenced by the ideology of the suzerainty treaty pattern as they sought to understand their covenant relationship with Yahweh. That assumption is no longer valid. Even the arguments that the eighth-century prophets were affected by more than the Decalogue and perhaps certain legal materials in the early books of Moses are arguments from silence. Only in the book of Deuteronomy does Israel make full use of the suzerainty treaty pattern with its appendix of curses and blessings. Against those who insist that an earlier appropriation of that treaty pattern would have been necessary in order that it be reflected in as late a document as Deuteronomy, I would reply simply: the full pattern may well have been known in Israel down to the seventh century without ever having been made normative in the religious tradition.

This development frees us to view the older portions of the Old Testament, including the Pentateuch (except Deuteronomy) and the eighth-century prophets, as material written without the background of the full treaty pattern with its powerful curses and blessings. The student of the earlier Pentateuchal materials and of the eighth-century prophets need not assume that God was thought to be more or less inevitably obliged by the covenant of his own making to retaliate in fixed measure against his erring people. Neither does the preacher whose task it is to develop a picture of the justice and the grace of God from these materials. Many episodes in the first four books of Moses and the prophets do not, after all, fit such a rigid scheme very well. For example, Ex. 16:27–29 and Hos. 11:1–9 each in different ways present God as able to transcend with compassion even situations which ought, in a treaty scheme, to have called forth his retributional wrath. By denying that the treaty pattern must always be presupposed from Sinai onward, we are perhaps freer to hear the Biblical writers affirm the truly sovereign and independent acts of grace by God which are not and cannot be related to the covenant obligations to bless and to curse.

The preceding discussion leads me to make a clear and confident assertion. Until the book of Deuteronomy wove earlier covenant traditions and the prophetic cries of judgment into a full-fledged legal covenant with sanctions, curse and blessing were not the framework preferred by Old Testament writers for understanding God's response to human activity. Nor was the motif of divine retribution the key to the understanding of human history. That the motif of divine retribution and the pattern of curse and blessing assume a greater interpretive importance in Biblical thought after the appearance of the book of Deuteronomy cannot be gainsaid. However, even there the literary strategy of a possible fresh start for Israel and the hint that the choice for obedience still remains open prevent the retributional theology of the work from becoming utterly rigid and simplistic. Repentance and change may still be possible. The full implementation of the curse may yet be held off for a little while!

Two Ways for Mankind

Text

1 Blessed is the man who walks not in the counsel of the
wicked, nor stands in the way of sinners, nor sits in the seat
of scoffers; 2 but his delight is in the law of the LORD, and on
his law he meditates day and night. 3 He is like a tree planted
by streams of water, that yields its fruit in its season, and its
leaf does not wither. In all that he does, he prospers. 4 The
wicked are not so, but are like chaff which the wind drives
away. 5 Therefore the wicked will not stand in the judgment,
nor sinners in the congregation of the righteous; 6 for the
LORD knows the way of the righteous, but the way of the
wicked will perish.

—*Psalm 1*

Discussion

The wisdom psalms,[30] sometimes called "the Psalms of the
Two Ways," are often taken to be the *locus classicus* in the
Old Testament for concise expression of retributional theology. Of these wisdom psalms, Psalm 1 is surely the most
familiar. The assurance of reward for the righteous and punishment for the wicked is the single message of the psalm.
The opening line identifies the psalm as a beatitude for the
righteous man. The Hebrew word translated by the English
"blessed" is not the word *bārūk,* which would be the usual
antonym of *'ārūr,* "cursed." Instead it is the word *'ashrē,*
which can also be translated "happy"! (NEB, JB). The happy
or blessed man is one who avoids evil company and spends
his time in "meditating" (v. 2) on the law of the Lord. The
Hebrew word used here for "meditates" could also be translated "recites." The picture is of a righteous Jew murmuring
as he thumbs his way through the pages of a *written* Torah.
This image suggests that this psalm is a relatively late reflection of Jewish piety.

The righteous man flourishes almost in the manner of the

eschatological tree of life (Ezek. 47:12; Rev. 22:2), a tree which never withers and which in all seasons yields good fruits of life for those who draw near. The wicked, in contrast, cannot stand effectively in the judgment nor in the congregation of the righteous. Whether this verse refers to a Last Judgment in which the "righteous" or the "saints" *(saddīqīm)* witness the great divine retribution against those who have opposed them and the will of God (see Dan. 12:2–3) or whether the reference is simply to an inevitable earthly judgment which awaits those who refuse to obey God cannot be determined absolutely.[31]

H.-J. Kraus[32] recognizes that the terms "judgment" and "congregation of the righteous" (v. 5) have eschatological overtones. His real interest, however, is to show that the psalm is written against the background of a struggle within Israel. The contrast between the "wicked" and the "righteous" is a contrast between those in the postexilic Jewish community who do not know that the Torah of Yahweh is wisdom and those observant "pious ones" who do. By cutting themselves off from the "wicked," the righteous protect the faith and gain their reward. For Kraus, the real thrust of the psalm is to illustrate the life of the *saddīq* in devotion to the Torah rather than to expand upon the fate of the wicked. The psalm can hardly be called a Psalm of the Two Ways, because only one way—the way of the righteous—is viable.

The theme of "the two ways" in the wisdom psalms is prominent throughout the Old Testament wisdom materials. It is no surprise that Klaus Koch, in a now-famous German article entitled "Is There a Dogma of Retribution in the Old Testament?"[33] focused on the wisdom tradition to support his thesis. Building on such passages as Prov. 26:27–28; 28:1, 10, 16b, 17–18, as well as texts from the wisdom psalms and elsewhere in the Psalter, Koch argued that the Old Testament tradition speaks frequently of requital from evil but does not insist that this requital is inflicted by God. In these texts, the evil deed seems to bring about its own unhappy

consequences almost as a law of nature. Koch finds in Proverbs no predetermined code of rewards and punishments for
deeds; rather, the relation of deed and result is more like that
of seed and harvest. He concludes that Proverbs has no real
doctrine of divine retribution, but rather a notion of "destiny-producing" human deeds. The same observation applies
to Psalm 1 and the other Psalms of the Two Ways.

Koch moves on to apply the thesis to the prophetic tradition. He does not attempt to deny that Yahweh provides the
providential context in which deeds and their effects continue in predictable relationship with each other. He does
argue that for the prophets, too, the proclamation of doom
is the proclamation that the consequences of sinful human
deeds are so inevitable that Yahweh cannot alter them. Yahweh can use these cause-and-effect sequences as a means of
correcting the people. But for the prophets, Kraus argues,
human deeds are generally understood to be producers of
their own destinies. In fact, the very language of the Old
Testament prophets, historians, and wise men links deed and
consequence. Kraus accepts the theory that the Old Testament has a dynamistic view of language which sees in the
very articulation of an idea or decision the setting in motion
of the forces which will bring that idea or decision to fulfillment.

Subsequent discussion of the Koch thesis has faulted the
argument in several ways.[34] Some critics have pointed out
Koch's lack of consideration of the Deuteronomic tradition
of interpreting history in categories of divine retribution.
Others have noted his neglect of the concept of lex talionis.
An all-encompassing thesis of the sort that Koch has advanced inevitably runs the danger either of forcing all evidence to fit the thesis in some way or another, or else of
ignoring data which cannot be easily accounted for. Both
criticisms have been leveled against Koch's discussion. Yet
another criticism is that Koch fails to take into account certain texts, particularly those in which Yahweh imposes a pen-

alty. Such texts present a punishment not as an automatic result of an evil deed but as a righteous sentence consciously imposed by a judge upon an injuring party. Finally, the thesis rests upon the assumption that Hebrew language is essentially dynamistic in its psychology. To the Biblical writers a word of cursing or of blessing always set in motion consequences which, once released, could no longer be controlled. James Barr has long since shown that this allegedly dynamistic conception of the Hebrew language cannot be sustained in a wide range of Old Testament texts.[35]

For all these criticisms, Koch's thesis continues to stimulate interpreters to relate larger theological motifs to the rather commonsensical and secular observation in those wisdom texts which speak of the direct relationship of human activities to fateful and inevitable consequences. "He who digs a pit will fall into it, and a stone will come back upon him who starts it rolling" (Prov. 26:27–28). A thesis such as that advanced by Koch may well account for at least some of these teachings. In so doing, it can limit the extent to which the motif of divine retribution must be assumed to permeate the wisdom tradition of the Old Testament.

Direction

To this point we have reviewed Old Testament materials which draw in one way or another upon the motif of retribution in order to lay an ideological basis for law, prophetic proclamation, the historical interpretation of events, and poetic theological reflection. We have discerned applications of the notion of retribution as a principle governing human and divine activity. We have also encountered the repeated suggestion that the very texts which trade upon the motif also contain within them features which can legitimately be understood to reduce the harshest aspects of the retributional scheme. They even open them out toward more inclusive theological frameworks for interpreting experience.

First, B. S. Jackson proposed that the *lex talionis* was inserted relatively late into its present setting in the older portion of Pentateuchal law (at Ex. 21:22–25). This would tend to eliminate the need to assume that basic retributional formula per se to be part of the theoretical background of all subsequent legal thought in ancient Israel. The same proposal of relative *lateness* also appears in recent thinking about the suzerainty treaty pattern as the basic form of covenant in early Israel. Perhaps the full suzerainty treaty pattern, with its divinely guaranteed sanctions of curse and blessing, had not yet become the theoretical model underlying all Mosaic and prophetic discussions of the God-man relationship. If so, it follows that one need not assume that the early theologians and prophets interpreted events and their consequences primarily in terms of the legally obligatory divine retribution that the suzerainty treaty pattern implies.

Second, I argued that an element which I called its *open-endedness* in the very literary form of the book of Deuteronomy suggests that the purpose of the book is not simply to interpret all of history, past, present, and future, in terms of divine retribution. Rather, it encourages the reader and the hearer to decide for obedience while time still remains. The evangelical thrust of Deuteronomy and even the Deuteronomic historical work with which it is associated is visible both in Deut. 30:20 and in II Kings 25:27–30. In the former, the people are called upon to choose the way of Yahweh and, in the literary fiction of the book of Deuteronomy, they are left on Jordan's bank at that very moment of decision. In the latter, the possibility of picking up the thread of blessing still seems open, if only because the curse has not been implemented absolutely.

Third, the concept of *"destiny-producing deeds"* advanced by Koch would tend to eliminate the motif of divine retribution almost entirely from consideration. Although the thesis has considerable difficulties, it may provide a different way of understanding some of the harshest and most simplistic wisdom teachings about the inevitability of disaster for those who practice evil. The effect is to suggest that evil deeds done in the ordinary course of human events bring about their own downfall.

Finally, in the Psalms of the Two Ways and elsewhere where the lives of the righteous and the wicked are contrasted, it may be *the righteous and their behavior* alone which are the central theme. This is the thesis of Kraus in dealing with Psalm 1. If the basic purpose of these psalms is simply to set the one authentic and life-giving Way over against the dark background of a non-way, then the assumption is blunted that the psalms are really written to illustrate the working of divine retribution.

These four limitations upon the elemental force of the motif of divine retribution are suggestive and deserve further reflection. They do not, however, by any means add up to an overcoming of the motif. It is and will be my contention that the motif cannot be overcome, because it is an integral part of the Old Testament. Indeed, the conviction that evil deeds have their day of reckoning and that disobedience to God's will does not lead to life but to death is a frequent and significant theme within the text of the entire Bible. However, it is also my thesis that this motif of divine retribution is not simply balanced by a contrapuntal motif of divine intention to redeem and save the world, but is actually embraced by it. But I run ahead of myself. This encompassing of the theme of divine retribution by the theme of divine redemption can only be shown after we have surveyed texts which illustrate the eschatological expression of the motif of divine retribution.

RETRIBUTION ON A COSMIC SCALE

Text

1 At that time shall arise Michael, the great prince who has charge of your people. And there shall be a time of trouble,

THE DIVINE "NO" IN THE BIBLE

such as never has been since there was a nation till that time; but at that time your people shall be delivered, every one whose name shall be found written in the book. 2 And many of those who sleep in the dust of the earth shall awake, some to everlasting life, and some to shame and everlasting contempt. 3 And those who are wise shall shine like the brightness of the firmament; and those who turn many to righteousness, like the stars for ever and ever.

—Daniel 12:1–3

Discussion

This is the only Old Testament text to refer unmistakably to a judgment day upon which the dead are resurrected and judged according to their mortal deeds. It can also be reliably dated to the very end of the Old Testament period. Scholars generally agree that the writer of Dan., chs. 7 to 12, was alive during the reign of the Seleucid king Antiochus (IV) Epiphanes (176–163 B.C.). In the seer's lengthy vision of 11:2 to 12:4, it is quite possible to trace the history of late Persian and Hellenistic Palestine from the rise of Alexander the Great (11:3) down to the struggles connected with Antiochus' sack of Jerusalem and desecration of the Temple in 167 B.C. (11:31). It is also commonly assumed that because the author of these chapters of Daniel witnessed the later events of these chapters with his own eyes the exact moment of the writing of the book can be determined. That moment can be located at the point at which the more or less factual recounting of events ends and predictions of actually unfulfilled future occurrences begin, namely, at 11:40. After this point, the seer's eyes are lifted slowly beyond the chaos of the end of this age to the turning of the new aeon. Chapter 12 describes the culmination of the eschatological moment, and introduces the concept of the Day of Judgment. All is to take place "at that time" (12:1), a time which can only be understood as a few years beyond 167 B.C. (see Dan. 9:24–27).

At that time, taught the seer, the angel Michael will arise
and all those among the people of the seer whose names
"shall be found written in the book" shall be delivered. This
book could have been familiar to the ancient hearers of the
seer as the eschatological book of remembrance, the book in
which the deeds of the people of Israel are written for good
or for ill (see Mal. 3:16). The phraseology of v. 2 suggests that
not all but only "many of those who sleep in the dust" shall
be raised. Following this resurrection some are awarded
everlasting life and some receive only "shame and everlasting contempt." "Those who are wise" (v. 3) are singled out
for special eschatological blessing. We may assume that these
"wise" *(maskīlīm)* are none other than the writer's own con-
stituency. A number of theories regarding the exact identity
of this group have been advanced. The one which seems to
have achieved greatest acceptance links them with the religiously observant and pietistic group of Hasidim who, according to I Macc. 2:42, joined the Jewish resistance to the
tyranny of Antiochus IV but later took a quietistic stand
(7:12–14).

The literary genre of the Book of Daniel is "apocalyptic."
Apocalyptic literature is a distinct subcategory within the
larger body of Biblical texts (mostly found in the prophetic
canon) which are described as "eschatological," i.e., having
to do with the Last Things *(eschaton,* "last"). The difference
between prophetic eschatology and apocalyptic writing at its
early stages can be seen if one compares Isa. 11:1–9, representing prophetic eschatology, with Zech. 14:1–9, representing early apocalyptic writing. Both of these texts present a
vision of the future in which certain fundamental changes
brought about by God's action guarantee to mankind a life
free of the tragedies of war, disaster, and death. However,
the Isaiah passage maintains a certain realism in its vision.
Even when it promises that known enemies within the ani-
mal kingdom will lie down together in total harmony, the
figures are still those of the well-known creatures of our own

experience. Kingship is still kingship, though righteous and wise to a degree hitherto unknown. The earth is still the earth, and the life which will be lived in it still has human feelings, joys, and satisfactions. In the Zechariah account, on the other hand, the eschatological changes are more nearly ontological in character. Valleys rise and mountains fall, and the cosmos itself is altered beyond recognition: ". . . there shall be continuous day . . . not day and not night. . . ." In short, eschatology maintains something more like a realistic vision of the promised restoration on the Day of the Lord, while apocalyptic moves beyond that vision into the heightened realm of the mythic.[36] The word "myth," in this sense, refers to the divine origin of realities that affect our lives and will continue to do so to the end of time. I would accept as a rough definition of "apocalyptic" literature the description "mythologized eschatology." S. Frost has identified four mythic themes in particular which impact upon the dramatic view of God's victory already presupposed by prophetic eschatology and move it in the direction of apocalyptic.[37] As they must do, these mythic themes recall not only the end but also the beginning of the world. The themes are the primordial struggle of creation; the vision of a paradise or golden age; the recognition of a king or messiah in that paradise; and the threat of a world catastrophe or judgment. Once these mythic themes infuse the prophetic vision of a restored and perfected future, the dimensions become cosmic, the struggle between good and evil becomes polarized almost to the point of dualism, and the fate of the enemies of God becomes associated not only with defeat and destruction but with the flaming hell of an eternal retribution.[38] Obviously, the degree to which apocalyptic literature moves the prophetic vision of a day of Yahweh's triumph over his enemies in the direction of a highly amplified day of Yahweh's retribution poses considerable difficulty for my thesis that world redemption, not hellfire, is God's ultimate purpose. Before this problem is examined, however, we need to return briefly to the question of the circles which gave rise to the apocalyptic literature. Who were the "wise"? Who were their pre-second-century B.C. predecessors? And what motivated them to think and write in the direction of ever more fully amplified apocalyptic scenario of divine retribution?

A recent writer on the subject, Paul Hanson, believes that the origin of Old Testament apocalyptic has to be seen in disillusioned prophetic and Levitical circles of the postexilic period.[39] Although most of the members of this party may never have been in the Babylonian captivity, they cherished a continuing expectation of the full implementation of Deutero-Isaiah's vision of a restored and perfected Israelite community in the Palestinian homeland. Increasingly, their hope threw them into antipathy to the spirit of the restoration carried out by the members of the temple establishment. The authors of apocalyptic are thus to be set over against the ruling priestly circles of Jerusalem and their writings preserved in Ezra-Nehemiah-Chronicles. Hanson sees the circles which gave rise to the apocalyptic literature not so much as a continuously identifiable visionary party, but as a succession of disenchanted, politically disenfranchised, and increasingly ahistorically oriented thinkers and writers.

A similar view of the setting-in-life out of which apocalyptic grows has been advanced by O. Plöger.[40] For Plöger, the origin of apocalyptic is to be sought in a postexilic, antiestablishment movement with Levitical character. He differs from Hanson partly in the fact that he is even willing to describe the movement as an ongoing party. They were Torah-true Jews whose worship, carried on in "underground" conventicles, maintained a burning eschatological expectation, as evidenced by liturgical elements still preserved in the apocalyptic writings. By hypothetical connections such as these, scholars seek to tie the eschatological expectation of the prophetic writers to the later canonical apocalyptic literature of the Old Testament, i.e., Daniel, Isa., chs. 24 to 27, Joel 2:28 to 3:21, and Zech., chs. 9 to 14. Such theories suggest that the prophetic notion of the vindication of the righteous and the checking of the wicked in historical events and by divine interventions was actually projected by apocalyptic onto the large screen of the cosmos to yield a retributional theology of cosmic, universal, and eternal proportions.

Direction

Much of our modern theological conception of The Retribution, the divine intervention at the end of time to reward the righteous and destroy the wicked, is derived from the apocalyptic literature of the Old and New Testaments. This brief sketch of the origin and growth of this literature has suggested possible ways in which theologians and the "wise" in Israel brought the motif of divine retribution from its relatively mundane expression in the Psalms of the Two Ways, the prophetic oracles of judgment, and the Deuteronomic history to the vast, cosmic form in which it appears in apocalyptic. But to have available a theoretical model for the literary history of the motif is not the same as finding a suitable way of relating that motif in its apocalyptic form to the thesis of this study, namely, that the retributional activity of God must ultimately be seen in the more inclusive Biblical context of God's redemptive purpose.

Apropos the place of apocalyptic in the larger context, I would make only two observations. First, I affirm its great importance in the Biblical tradition as well as to the faith. It is important not simply for the light which it sheds upon the motif of divine retribution, and not simply as a theology for hard times which can assure the beleaguered saints of the punishment of their enemies and their own reward.[41] Far more than these, apocalyptic expresses the great and perennial expectation of a theodicy, a stunning moment in which God shows that his way of dealing with evil is the right way and in which all the kings and peoples of the earth recognize his greatness and confess his name. Apocalyptic literature also positively affirms that because all our present days stand in the shadow of that future divine self-vindication, people of goodwill can get on with the business of living now as participants in the Kingdom of Heaven. Of these claims we shall speak later.

Second, I must at this point categorically assert that as a map of the future and a detailed account of factual matters regarding the coming events of history, the Old Testament apocalyptic writings are of no value. Like any other Biblical tradition couched in symbolic terms, apocalyptic literature requires demythologization and re-expression in analogous but contemporary language before it can be meaningful in the shaping of the Christian progress into the future. This applies to the details recorded in Dan. 12:1–3: the angel, the record book, the Retribution, and everlasting contempt. We shall have yet additional occasions to consider the eschatological dimension of the motif of divine retribution and to assess its place alongside the Biblical motif of divine redemption. But at all points I will insist that the kerygma of God's power to fulfill his purpose be affirmed separately from the colorful narrative vehicle in which that kerygma is carried.

THE BEAUTIFUL AND THE DAMNED

Text

> 1 Then I saw an angel coming down from heaven, holding in his hand the key of the bottomless pit and a great chain. 2 And he seized the dragon, that ancient serpent, who is the Devil and Satan, and bound him for a thousand years, 3 and threw him into the pit, and shut it and sealed it over him, that he should deceive the nations no more, till the thousand years were ended. After that he must be loosed for a little while.

4 Then I saw thrones, and seated on them were those to whom judgment was committed. Also I saw the souls of those who had been beheaded for their testimony to Jesus and for the word of God, and who had not worshiped the beast or its image and had not received its mark on their foreheads or their hands. They came to life, and reigned with Christ a thousand years. 5 The rest of the dead did not come to life until the thousand years were ended. This is the first resurrection. 6 Blessed and holy is he who shares in the first resurrection! Over such the second death has no power, but they shall be priests of God and of Christ, and they shall reign with him a thousand years.

7 And when the thousand years are ended, Satan will be loosed from his prison 8 and will come out to deceive the nations which are at the four corners of the earth, that is, Gog and Magog, to gather them for battle; their number is like the sand of the sea. 9 And they marched up over the broad earth and surrounded the camp of the saints and the beloved city; but fire came down from heaven and consumed them, 10 and the devil who had deceived them was thrown into the lake of fire and brimstone where the beast and the false prophet were, and they will be tormented day and night for ever and ever.

11 Then I saw a great white throne and him who sat upon it; from his presence earth and sky fled away, and no place was found for them. 12 And I saw the dead, great and small, standing before the throne, and books were opened. Also another book was opened, which is the book of life. And the dead were judged by what was written in the books, by what they had done. 13 And the sea gave up the dead in it, Death and Hades gave up the dead in them, and all were judged by what they had done. 14 Then Death and Hades were thrown into the lake of fire. This is the second death, the lake of fire; 15 and if any one's name was not found written in the book of life, he was thrown into the lake of fire.

—*Revelation 20:1–15*

Discussion

Many contemporary scholars do not find the themes of cosmic catastrophe and the Day of Judgment strongly emphasized in the preaching of Jesus, although the motif of Kingdom of Heaven in his preaching provides a link to the apocalyptic tradition. Jesus' own consciousness is of a burning nearness of the Kingdom; there is an urgency in his summons to prepare to enter that Kingdom. But the development of apocalyptic thought beyond what was current in the Judaism of the time, and therefore further articulation of the motif of divine retribution, is not the work of Jesus. It is only in the aftermath of the resurrection that the church begins to discover its faith in the Second Coming, or Parousia, of the Son of Man. As this Parousia becomes a focal point of preaching about the future, it also becomes associated—perhaps through the image of the Son of Man as known already in Dan. 7:13–14 and the post-canonical Jewish book of Enoch[42] —with the themes of a general resurrection of the dead and Last Judgment. P. Vielhauer[43] treats the larger apocalyptic sections in the Epistles and the Gospels under the heading "dogmatizing of apocalyptic ideas." He regards these as relatively later stages in the development of New Testament tradition. Under this heading he includes II Peter and the "little apocalypses" in Matt., chs. 24 to 25, Mark, ch. 13, and Luke 21:5–36. The Johannine apocalypse represents an even further development in New Testament apocalyptic thinking. By this reckoning, it would indicate the state of early Christian theological reflection on the End at least two steps removed from Jesus himself. In Revelation we arrive at the final stage of development of the Biblical motif of divine retribution. I have chosen this passage from Rev., ch. 20, as illustrative of the stage.

The events of the Last Day and The Retribution presented in the book of Revelation are difficult to describe exactly. Bornkamm[44] perceives a threefold presentation of the apocalyptic drama. In his view the same events are described first in the vision of the seals (6:1 to 8:1), then in a preparatory way (8:2 to 14:20) and in a final way (15:1 to 20:15). Although other outlines of the book of Revelation have also been advanced, suffice it to say that all recognize ch. 20 as containing the Last Judgment, the *penultimate* event of the eschatological series, and the act just prior to the revelation of the New Jerusalem. Since this phase of the apocalyptic vision is most important for my effort to understand the motif of divine retribution in its cosmic setting, a brief discussion of the details of this text now follows.

Scene one of this last section of the apocalyptic scenario is contained in 20:1–3. An angel captures Satan and imprisons him in a bottomless pit for one thousand years. The bottomless pit or abyss is not to be identified with the lake of fire (vs. 14–15), nor with Hades (vs. 13–14). Each seems to refer to some separate dimension of the writer's conception of the underworld. In contrast, the devil, Satan, the dragon, and the ancient serpent are all identified with each other even though an examination of other texts in and out of the Bible can show that each term has a separate prehistory. The idea of a thousand-year imprisonment of Satan, also understood as a phase between the appearance of the Messiah and the final judgment, has a prior history in Jewish eschatology as well. The figure of one thousand years is not always intrinsic to the notion. In II Esdras 7:26–42, for example, the Messiah appears, rules four hundred years, then dies. The seven days of silence which follow his death culminate in a general resurrection and the judgment. It is worth noting, however, that the concept of a millennium appears nowhere else in the New Testament.

The second event in this last chapter in history is reported in 20:4–6. Simultaneously with the binding of Satan a first resurrection of martyrs who had been beheaded for their testimony to Jesus (v. 4) takes place, and these rule with Christ for a thousand years. I find it impossible to determine from these verses whether the writer thought the martyrs would reign with Christ in heaven or whether they would be physically present with him on earth. The latter possibility seems to be borne out by the reference to "the camp of the saints and the beloved city" in v. 9; however, it is not necessary to identify the "saints" of v. 9 with the "beheaded" of v. 4. The old heaven and the old earth are not removed until v. 11, so at least the possibility exists that the events reported in 20:4–10 are seen as taking place in this world. Another obscurity, too, confronts the interpreter in this second act of the drama of ch. 20. Verse 4 implies that the martyrs and Christ collectively are "those to whom judgment was committed." However, v. 11 finds no judge at work except the one who sits upon the great white throne, apparently eliminating the martyrs and possibly even Christ from the actual acts of Last Judgment.

The third stage in the drama of the final judgment is contained in 20:7–10. After one thousand years, Satan is unbound from the abyss and, with Gog and Magog (who are the nations at the four corners of the earth), attacks the saints and the beloved city. In this battle the devil and his followers are defeated and thrown into the lake of fire for the last time. The final events are pictured in 20:11, 12–15. First, the present earth and sky flee away from the presence of him who sits upon the great white throne of judgment, and the way is cleared for a new heaven and a new earth. The actual second judgment takes place in vs. 12–15. It is not absolutely clear here who is sitting upon the great white throne. In some Jewish apocalyptic texts the Son of Man does the judging on the Last Day. The same teaching is implicit in Luke 21:27 and explicit in Matt. 25:31–46. The fact that God judges from the throne in Dan. 7:9–14, a passage which obviously underlies the picture being drawn here, seems to be the strongest evidence in favor of understanding him as the judge in 20:12.

The relationship between what the resurrected dead had done during their lifetimes and a final judgment is established by means of the "books" which are opened on the occasion. One might see in the opening of the "books" and the judgment rendered according to their evidence the climactic point of the motif of divine retribution in the Bible. We have already encountered the divine record book in Dan. 12:1. However, for the first time in any of the canonical apocalyptic writings a second book is also present. A book "which is the book of life" finally determines who will be saved and who will be cast into the lake of fire (v. 15). The relation of the record books to the book of life is not made clear. Perhaps the writer thought that a transfer would be made at the end of an individual's lifetime or at the Eschaton by which that person's record would be indicated in the book of life by the inscription or omission of the person's name— a kind of heavenly double-entry bookkeeping system. No Scriptural evidence for such a step exists, however. Inasmuch as earlier Biblical references to the heavenly "book" understand it in at least two distinct ways, we may assume that the writer maintains something of both understandings by visualizing two kinds of books here. Some references to the "book" elsewhere in Revelation (Rev. 3:5; 21:27), the only other reference to the image in the New Testament (Phil. 4:3; the reference in Heb. 10:7 is a citation of Ps. 40:7), and a number of Old Testament references (Ex. 32:32–33; Ps. 40:7; 56:8; 69:28; Dan. 7:10; 12:1; Mal. 3:16) all seem to point toward a juridical concept of a record book in which individual good and evil deeds are recorded. Other texts, in contrast, regard the book as containing God's plan for his creation, perhaps written before the beginning of time (Ps. 139:16; Rev. 13:8; 17:8). If the latter theme is present in this passage at all, it would seem that "the book of life" would be more likely to record the eternal decree of God, while "the books" would contain the records compiled by individuals upon which the basis of divine retribution is to be meted out. Even if the two "books" have distinguishable functions at the judgment, their relationship to one another at the point of decision-making is unclear. What is clear is the fate of those whose names are not written in the book of life: they are thrown into the lake of fire, together with Death and Hades themselves. Sinners forever tormented in the lake of fire! On this note ends the motif of divine retribution, now projected into the cosmic dimension by the apocalyptic scenario of world catastrophe and judgment.

Direction

It is impossible to say precisely what the seer of Patmos wanted to affirm about certain details of the Eschaton. It is impossible to harmonize everything he said, even in the book of Revelation itself, into one neatly unified apocalyptic scheme. It is even more difficult to coordinate that with the picture painted by the rest of the apocalyptic materials of the New Testament. However, the message of Rev., ch. 20, is strong enough to lead us to believe that the writer meant what he said, although he did not say with entire clarity what he meant. He meant to say that the last act to take place before the descent of the New Jerusalem from heaven and from God as a bride adorned for her husband must be the destruction of all those whose deeds were not consonant with the purity and perfection of that new order. This is the hardest and fiercest statement of the motif of divine retribution to be found in the entire Bible. Yet it is simply the end point of a trajectory which was already clear in Old Testament apocalyptic texts and incipient even in earlier prophetic and legal traditions. Our studies of these earlier traditions have suggested the presence within them of restrictions on and mitigations of the harshest aspects of the motif. Still, the major line of development of the motif within the Bible does in fact culminate in this apocalyptic vision of the destruction of a substantial portion of the creation in a lake of fire to the glory of God and the maintenance of perfect divine justice. How can such a denouement be related to my thesis that the Biblical motif of divine retribution is properly to be seen in connection with and finally in subordination to the motif of God's purpose to redeem the entire cosmos and all its creatures?

I would begin responding to this problem by reiterating the point already stated. In the light of the patently surrealistic mode of expression in apocalyptic, we must affirm that the details of the great apocalyptic drama are of no significance to us as projective historical data. Even though we want to continue to assert that God will vindicate his way of dealing with evil and injustice in the world at the moment of the culmination of his purpose, these texts really cannot tell us how he will do it. This principle must be invoked every time someone comes up with the latest article or sensational paperback best-seller proving that all census figures in the last twenty years can be related via computer to the number of the beast, or some such nonsense. The number of the beast, the lake of fire, the thousand years, and all other details are of no use to us in predicting or describing the events of the future. This we shall have to affirm even though we know that the writer of Revelation intended to the best of his knowledge and using the best imagery that was available to him to give us an accurate description of what he thought was going to happen relatively soon.

We believe this literature has extraordinary value to faith, however, not only because it is canonical Scripture but also because of the richness which the substantial truth-claims of its message promise to add to our understanding of God's way of dealing with his world. So, we will still want to take it seriously. We will have to begin by cutting the tie between the vision and the actual history of the future, by saying, "We do not think this is a literal account of future events but that it is an account of something else." We will have to recognize apocalyptic literature as theology-writing, not history-writing. Our task will then be to penetrate through the detailed apocalyptic scenario to the kerygma of Revelation, reconstructing the message of apocalyptic along lines that believers can read and understand. The motif of divine retribution will be a part, indeed one of the essential teachings, of this kerygma. There will be other elements as well: the assurance of the ultimate triumph of God; the hope, based on this assurance, in which the believer marches into the future; the dynamic view of history which says as loudly as possible, "Time marches on!" We will have occasion to look again at this kerygmatic approach to Biblical apocalyptic and its implications for a proper understanding of the motif of divine retribution during our second cycle through the Scriptures.

To place the focus upon the *kerygma* of the Biblical apocalyptic literature rather than upon the details of the scenario still does not per se relieve us from the burden of proof. For one who would argue that the Biblical word of the success of God's retributional activity is not the last Biblical word, further support is needed.

One way of developing such further support will be to ask (as I shall do in Chapter IV), "Have we fully understood the writer's intent in Rev., ch. 20?" Although the plain meaning of 20:14–15 is retribution in a lake of fire against all whose names are not written in the book of life, is there possibly a sequel to this event in ch. 21? One encouragement toward asking such a question comes from the Epistles. Paul, who certainly is thoroughly familiar with the outlines of the apocalyptic thought that is later more fully developed in Revelation, seems to be aware of the possibility of such a sequel. (I Cor. 15:28. See my treatment of the matter, below, pp. 128 ff.)

With such a step, however, yet another problem arises. What warrant has an interpreter who seeks to assess the relative weight or priority of two such pervasive Biblical motifs as divine retribution and divine redemption deliberately to choose to use certain texts as offering more essential support for his thesis rather than others? I shall explore this question in more detail in Chapter III. For the moment I shall simply state that, in my judgment, Paul's "sequel" to the final act of judgment accords better with the testimony of the Word to whom the Scriptures bear witness. That incarnate Word, the resurrected Lord against whose judgment, execution, and vindication all other words of Scripture must be measured, provides the key to the relative theological priority of the Biblical motifs of retribution and redemption, and therefore, by implication, the key to deciding which really has the *last* word.

Chapter III

RELATING THE DIVINE "NO"
TO THE DIVINE "YES"

THE DAMNING SYNTHESIS

Throughout the ages, Christian preachers and teachers have sought a synthesis on the subject of divine retribution. They have sought to incorporate the many texts of the Bible which bear upon the subject into a single unified whole which can then be set forth as "the Biblical teaching about God, the judge and retributor." Such an approach is not concerned to maintain the nuances and distinctions between the various texts which bear on the theme, but, on the contrary, to eliminate such distinctions. Such a synthesis has often then been incorporated into an entire systematic theological system, with the assumption that whatever the Bible teaches about the matter of divine retribution is not finally irreconcilable with other theological motifs similarly synthesized from Biblical materials. The result of the entire transaction can vary with the outlook and predisposition of the interpreter. The general outline, however, of the orthodox "Biblical" and dogmatic position regarding the matter of divine retribution for human sin looks something like the following:

Just as happiness and success can be seen by the eyes of faith as rewards, so suffering can often be accounted for as divine punishment for sin. Other accounts are possible, accounts that would discern in the suffering and disaster of our lifetimes divine testing and teaching.

But the probationary and pedagogical interpretations yield ultimately to the retributional interpretation, especially when the question of eternal reward-and-punishment is addressed. Eternal reward is possible for those who confess faith in Jesus Christ and repent of their sins. For those who do not confess their faith in Jesus Christ or having confessed belief in him nonetheless fail to repent and live a new life, divine retribution and everlasting punishment are in store.

The synthetic approach feels free to draw upon Deuteronomic theology, the teachings of the Psalms of the Two Ways, and the New Testament apocalyptic materials to make the simple link between obedience and belief with earthly reward and eternal salvation on the one hand, and disobedience and unbelief with punishment and damnation on the other.

This reductionistic treatment of the multiple and complex Biblical witness to the motif of divine retribution is perhaps most visible in the classical confessional statements of the Protestant churches. All confessions are summaries not only of Biblical teaching but of a long history of doctrinal discussion as well. Still, their claim to authority hinges substantially upon their success at demonstrating fidelity to the Scriptural witness. Confessions ought therefore to be considered whenever the question at hand has to do with the way Biblical data are appropriated by the believing community. I have included this brief treatment of confessional statements on divine retribution because the confessions—or popular interpretation of them—continue to exert a powerful influence in shaping Christian thought at a very basic level. I am convinced that all Christian believers draw most importantly upon two resources in making our day-to-day theological judgments. These are, in order of importance, (1) our knowledge of the Bible and (2) the memory of our catechesis, whether it be the simple teaching "at our mother's knee" or church school and confirmation experiences which we had as children. The power of the simple epitome of the faith represented by creedal statements lies precisely in its ability to state essential doctrine with a succinct eloquence. That such terse and memorable formulations do violence to the diversity of Biblical tradition yields to the important task of mediating theology to persons who are not assumed to have a high standard of theological sophistication. This can be illustrated in confessional statements of the "doctrine" of divine retribution, ultimately derived from such texts as we have reviewed in Chapter II. Paragraphs dealing with the issue are cited from a Lutheran and a Reformed confession. Both concentrate on the eschatological dimension of divine reward-and-punishment; in both, the nature of The Retribution is stated precisely, clearly, and unambiguously.

The first section is Chapter XVII of the Augsburg Confession of 1530, entitled "The Return of Christ to Judgment."

> It is also taught among us that our Lord Jesus Christ will return on the last day for judgment and will raise up all the dead, to give eternal life and everlasting joy to believers and the elect but to condemn ungodly men and the devil to hell and eternal punishment.
>
> Rejected, therefore, are the Anabaptists who teach that the devil and condemned men will not suffer eternal pain and torment.
>
> Rejected, too, are certain Jewish opinions which are even now making an appearance and which teach that, before the resurrection of the dead, saints and godly men will possess a worldly kingdom and annihilate all the godless.[1]

The Augsburg Confession was designed to find middle ground between Catholics on the one hand and the radical reformers on the other. It represented Melanchthon's best effort to state for the emperor Charles V and the German public at large the essence of the Lutheran faith. The treatment of the divine retribution at the Last Judgment is included in the first section of the Confession, which is a summary of twenty-one central articles of the faith of Lutheranism. The apocalyptic scenario of The Retribution, which we have already examined in the form in which it appears in Rev. 20:1–15, is compressed into a single act of resurrection and judgment (not the two of 20:4 and 20:12). In apparent conflict with Rev. 20:4–6, the Confession specifically rejects the "Jewish" notion of a millennial kingdom in which the saints and godly men will rule. On the other hand, the Confession makes it clear that the judge upon the throne of judgment (Rev. 20:11) is none other than the Lord Jesus Christ. The possibility of universal salvation, a teaching which is attributed to certain Anabaptists,[2] is specifically rejected.

In summary, the picture of The Retribution presented in the Augsburg Confession XVII has considerably simplified the witness of Rev., ch. 20. Exegetical problems have been solved without supporting evidence; details deemed extraneous have been simply eliminated. Above all, the dynamic tension which exists within the Bible itself between the retributional texts and other Biblical texts which also bear upon the subject of the eschatological moment is eliminated. I refer to the range of texts which suggest the possibility of a victory by God even over the sin and the disobedience of the large portion of the world, and the fulfillment of the divine purpose of redemption.

The Westminster Confession of Faith, written in 1644–1646, is "a magnificent statement of the faith in its particular context."[3] It was an effort to give clear definition to the Reformed faith which was dominant in England during the brief period of the English revolution. As was the case with the Augsburg Confession, the principal treatment of the motif of divine retribution deals with its eschatological form. Chapter XXXII, "On the State of Man After Death, and of the Resurrection of the Dead," teaches that after death the souls of the righteous are received immediately into heaven where they await the resurrection of their bodies. The souls of the wicked, on the other hand, are cast into hell, where they await the Judgment Day. Chapter XXXIII, "Of the Last Judgment," follows immediately.

1. God hath appointed a day wherein he will judge the world in righteousness by Jesus Christ, to whom all power and judgment is given of the Father; in which day, not only the apostate angels shall be judged; but likewise all persons that have lived upon earth shall appear before the tribunal of Christ, to give an account of their thoughts, words, and deeds; and to receive according to what they have done in the body, whether good or evil.

2. The end of God's appointing this day is for the manifestation of the glory of his mercy, in the eternal salvation of the elect; and of his justice, in the damnation of the reprobate, who are wicked and disobedient. For then shall the righteous go into everlasting life, and receive that fullness of joy and refreshing which shall come from the presence of the Lord; but the wicked, who know not God, and obey not the gospel of Jesus Christ, shall be cast into eternal torments, and be punished with everlasting destruction from the presence of the Lord, and from the glory of his power.

3. As Christ would have us to be certainly persuaded that there shall be a day of judgment, both to deter all men from sin and for the greater consolation of the godly in their adversity, so will he have that day unknown to men, that they may shake off all carnal security and be always watchful, because they know not at what hour the Lord will come, and may be ever prepared to say, "Come, Lord Jesus, come quickly." Amen.

As in the Augsburg Confession, this treatment of The Retribution is based primarily upon Rev., ch. 20. Once again, however, awkward details are eliminated and new elements added. The first paragraph, for example, makes reference to the "apostate angels" who will be judged before the throne of Christ, presumably at the moment visualized in Rev. 20: 12. The juridical examination of the dead is oral; no mention is made of the heavenly books. The second paragraph outlines the predestinarian idea of the eternal decree of God in its application to the Last Judgment. The salvation of the elect and the damnation of the reprobate are "for the manifestation of his [God's] mercy . . . and of his justice" respectively. The framers of the Westminster Confession moved well beyond the scope of the text of Revelation at this point to view The Retribution as a theodicy and to understand the purpose of the eschatological judgment to be the glorification of God in the first instance. The predestinarian modulation in Westminster's interpretation of The Retribution undoubtedly derives from the Calvinistic effort to deal seriously with the Pauline election theme (Rom. 8:29), as well as other Biblical references to God's prior decrees (Ps. 139:16; Acts 13:48). The idea of double predestination is, of course, essential to the Westminster Confession (see Ch. III). It is brought in here even though the bearing of God's eternal decree upon the record of good and evil "thoughts, words and deeds" compiled by every individual at the hour of judgment is quite problematical.[4] Difficult as this logical problem may seem to us today, it can at least be said that the Westminster divines recognized the existence of another strand of Biblical teaching which had a bearing upon the ultimate retributional act of God. They wove it into their statement on the Judgment Day. To this degree their Confession maintains more of the nuance and diversity of the Biblical treatment of the motif of divine retribution in its apocalyptic setting than does the Augsburg Confession. The American Declaratory Statement of 1903,[5] however, made a mishmash of the effort of the Westminster Confession to tie God's eternal decree to the retributional aspect of the Judgment Day. This Statement holds that the doctrine of God's eternal decree is in harmony with his freely offered gift of salvation to all men and that "no man is condemned except on the ground of his sin." As a corollary the Statement asserts that the Confession is not to be regarded as teaching that any who die in infancy are damned. In this additional note, American Calvinists recognized yet another Biblical motif which bears upon the matter of God's action in the eschatological events: the redemption

motif with its emphasis on God's love of all of his creation, the
assertion that God has "no pleasure in the death of any one"
(Ezek. 18:32), and that no man is condemned except on the
grounds of his own sin (Ezek. 18:20). The incorporation of
these themes is fair enough! And yet their presence in an
appendix to a confession creates a complexity which runs
against the very purpose of an epitome of the faith, even
though the result may be truer to the diversity of the Scripture itself.

Before proceeding to a critique of both the method and
the content of these synthetic treatments of the Biblical motif of divine retribution, particularly in its eschatological
form, I feel it appropriate to review another recent dogmatic
treatment of the doctrine. This review will illustrate the
problems which theology encounters in dealing with even
this one aspect of the complex Biblical motif of divine retribution. Harry Buis' book, *The Doctrine of Eternal Punishment*,[6] represents the effort of one contemporary writer to
defend that view of divine retribution in its eschatological
form which is contained in the confessions which we have
just reviewed. Although precritical in much of its Biblical
work and conservative in its aim, it gives more recognition
of the diversity of the Scriptural and historical discussions
underlying the position. I have selected this book for special
attention in preference to more substantial and scholarly
treatments,[7] largely because I believe its views are not far
removed from the opinions of great numbers of practicing
Christians of all denominations.

Buis begins his book with a sketch of the Old Testament
concept of Sheol, "a shadowy limited existence compared to
this life, but a very real existence."[8] Buis shows that Sheol was
conceived of as a place of darkness, silence, forgetfulness,
and separation—but nonetheless a place of continued existence. More important are Old Testament passages which
Buis believes point definitely to a future life—Gen. 22:5 (as
he believes it to be understood in Heb. 11:19), Job 19:25–27

(without dealing with the numerous technical problems with the passage), and Ps. 16:9b–11; 17:15; 49:12–15; and 75:24–26. Only a few Old Testament passages, in his view, definitely point to a future retribution; these include Dan. 12:2 and Isa. 24:21. This evidence can be summed up, however, in the conviction that one can legitimately extrapolate from the Old Testament view of divine reward-and-punishment to a concept of eternal life for the righteous and eternal death for the wicked.

Buis rightly shows that the great development in thinking about eschatological retribution takes place in the intertestamental period, particularly in Jewish apocalyptic literature. However, it is the New Testament that develops the doctrine to the full state which subsequent Christianity regards as normative for faith. Buis contends that "the loving and wise Savior has more to say about hell than any other individual in the Bible."[9] He quotes a statement from Shedd's *Dogmatic Theology* (1888) to the effect that "Jesus Christ is the person who is responsible for the doctrine of eternal perdition."[10] In support of these contentions he cites numerous examples, particularly from the Gospel of Matthew. Christ uses the words "hell" or "fire" and teaches that some will be sentenced to perish there at The Retribution.[11] Although some of Jesus' language about hell and heaven must be figurative (e.g., how can hell be both fire and darkness?), Buis does not doubt that Jesus taught the doctrine of divine retribution. His contemporaries, though wrong in accepting some of the extraordinary detail of Jewish apocalyptic faith, were nevertheless correct in believing in the existence of Gehenna and the possibility of damnation.

Moving on to Paul, Buis finds that the apostle reveals much less about the future state than Jesus does. However, because of the seriousness of his mission and because of specific, if brief, discussions of retribution (II Thess. 1:6–9) we can assume that he was deeply committed to the notion of divine retribution at least at the eschatological judgment.[12] Buis closes his review of the Biblical materials dealing with the eschatological dimension of divine retribution with this statement: "The orthodox doctrine of inspiration and the doctrine of eternal punishment stand or fall together. The only way to escape the doctrine of eternal punishment is to deny the infallibility of Scripture, and to deny that it is the one rule of faith and practice, which is historically a cardinal doctrine of Protestant churches."[13]

Buis' book goes on to give a useful summary of the attitudes of Christian theologians from the patristic period down to modern times toward the matter of divine, eschatological retribution. If nothing else, this history shows how ancient is the argument between those who deny any ultimate and final separation between the good and the evil and those who hold to the centrality of this doctrine to the Christian faith. Finally, he sums up the present-day conservative position on the matter. Conservatives believe in the doctrine of eternal punishment because the Bible teaches it; a theological doctrine without hell is morally dangerous; although modern conservatives repudiate the gross expression of hell in the literature of the Middle Ages and recognize that most of the imagery of the texts dealing with it is figurative, they affirm its real existence. Unlike theologians as long ago as Tertullian, modern conservatives do not look upon the suffering of sinners in hell as a cause for joy, but rather as a matter of sadness. Just as there are degrees of blessedness in heaven, so there are degrees of punishment in hell, according to the level of mortal sin. The locality of hell and heaven are unknown. Finally, the doctrine of hell undergirds missionary effort. "Those who are not saved now in the few years we have to work with them will be lost forever, they will spend eternity in hell, as God's word so plainly teaches."[14]

A Critique

My criticism of the work of Buis, of the sometimes literalistic, sometimes reductionistic viewpoint of which it is representative, and of the historic Protestant confessions themselves, begins at this point. Even in cases where writers have been careful not to impute a total unity of viewpoint to the Bible, there seems to be an assumption of an underlying Scriptural "right answer." In Buis' book, just as in the chapters on divine retribution in the Confessions, the real possibility of conflicting Scriptural points of view is never fully resolved. Leaving aside for the moment the question of whether Biblical criticism has validly shown that points of view attributed to Old Testament writers, and even to Jesus, are actually not from them but from later theological circles and editors, there is still a failure to take seriously the full diversity of Scriptural witness. Buis argues for the infallibility of Scripture, but simply echoes the position of the Westminster Confession and, for that matter, the Augsburg Confession. Yet he ignores such passages as Rom. 11:32; I Cor. 3:13–15; 15: 20–28; I John 4:17–18. These Scriptures, too, bear upon the question of divine retribution, and especially the matter of eternal reward-and-punishment. They do so just as validly as those upon which he has built his case for a universal assize in which the earthly deeds of persons are rewarded or punished with an eternal judgment. The Confessions, Buis, and other representatives of the older theological orthodoxy seem to feel that if one adopts the position that divine retribution is the key to understanding the destiny of obedient and disobedient mankind, then all other ways of understanding that destiny must be excluded. The reluctance to allow the Scripture to be seen in all of its meaningful diversity renders the treatment of the motif of divine retribution which traditional dogmatics offers less faithful and therefore less useful than is necessary for our times.

In fact, the assumption of a verbal inspiration, and therefore total internal harmony, of the Scriptures has long since been shown to be insupportable. If plenary inspiration is a wrong approach to the Scriptures, then the interpreter is left free to weigh and assess the interrelationship and relative importance of motifs such as divine retribution and universal redemption as they are raised explicitly or implicitly within the Bible. He is not bound, as the confession writers and orthodox interpreters feel they are, to maintain the imagery of damnation and retribution in an absolute way against all other metaphors for God's love and justice, even if the language of judgment appears to predominate in a particular portion of Scripture.

Another series of criticisms of the unified and synthetic summary presented in the confessions and the dogmatic manuals comes from the side of simple theological sense. Ordinary human realities make nonsense of the claim that the Deuteronomic curse-and-blessing scheme and its apocalyptic magnification is "the Biblical view." The Bible is an eminently human document. It is thoroughly aware of the realities of human fear, need, guilt, and the propensity to condemn those outside the pale of the righteous sect. Thus, it seems unlikely that a notion of divine retribution as rationalistic and rigid as that synthesized by the older confessions would accurately represent the full dimensions of the Biblical treatment of the theme. To assert that such a notion is "Biblical" overlooks the Christological center of Scripture with its passionate conviction that God's purpose has to do with redemption and salvation rather than damnation. To this "center" we will return in the following chapter.

Commonsense criticism of the "Biblical" summary presented in the older theological documents also points out the obvious morality in the behavior and faith of many outside the community of Christian believers. Even though the position may have some Biblical support (John 14:6; Acts 26:18), it does not make complete Biblical sense to assert categorically that such persons must experience the pain of divine retribution simply because they have not made formal profession of belief in the Lordship of Christ. (How does Paul put it? "Then as one man's trespass led to condemnation for all men, so one man's act of righteousness leads to acquittal and life for all men" [Rom. 5:18].) It does not make simple theological sense to deny *a priori* that there may be a congruence between their cause and the Christian vision of the Kingdom of Heaven.

Yet another commonsense criticism of this synthetic approach to the Biblical data of the theme of divine retribution has to do with its failure to recognize the limits of human religious knowledge. Separated from its primary function as witness to the one Word of God, incarnate in the person of Jesus Christ, the Bible is a human document. It is therefore open to both diversity and misinterpretation. Perhaps the real reason that traditional theology past and present has maintained the doctrine of divine retribution to be a univocal witness really has to do with the fear that a dilution of a vivid picture of the terrors of divine retribution, both now and in the hereafter, would undercut morality. Buis acknowledges as much, and the same assertion is often repeated in our own time.[15] There have been times in church history in which those who held to the importance of the deterrent force of the notion of retribution have—like the opponents of Galileo—asserted the doctrine even against demonstrable counterclaims. It was deemed necessary to curb dangerous innovations and prevent disorder.

A final objection to the retributional dogma outlined above is that eternal punishment for temporal sins, no matter how gross, is excessive and unrealistic. It cannot adequately reflect the realistic appraisal of the human situation contained in many and diverse forms in Scripture. Eternal punishment does not fit the temporal crime. Such a doctrine tends to measure our own fallible conceptions of justice and goodness, which are essentially cultural and relational in character, against pure attributes of God which cannot really be properly conceived of at all and of which the Bible has remarkably little to say. The result is that the abstract notion of God's absolute justice pushes dogmatics in the direction of saying that if human justice requires the punishment of human sin and evil, how much more does transcendent and absolute justice (understandable only as human justice raised to the nth power) require punishment (also raised to the nth power). Such an argument actually does not follow. Even the essentially untestable notion of God's absolute justice can be maintained without the syllogism given above. The absolute and holy justice of God might just as well be a justice which overcomes evil with the totality of its goodness.

FIVE PRINCIPLES OF INTERPRETATION

The time has come to turn from this critique of the traditional dogmatic appropriation of the Biblical data bearing upon the theme of God as one who rewards and punishes to a positive statement of a better mode of interpretation. I will begin with a statement of general principles, expressed in the form of propositions. The concluding paragraphs of this section will discuss the application of these principles specifically to the topic of this study. My hope is that this exercise will not only indicate a way in which the motif of divine retribution can best be understood, but will also illustrate an adequate method for dealing with any ubiquitous and diversely expressed Biblical motif.

Thesis One
From the aesthetic point of view, many Biblical texts deal with the motif of divine retribution "work"; from the theological point of view the motif points to an indispensable aspect of the word of God. There is no question about the literary effectiveness of the grand apocalyptic drama in the book of Revelation, or of the smaller depictions of divine

retribution in other Biblical passages. Examples include the powerful curses of Deut., ch. 27, the memorable cadences of Psalm 1, the parable of the wise and foolish maidens (Matt. 25:1–13), or the parable of Lazarus and Dives (Luke 16: 19–31). These texts "work," in the sense that they capture the imagination of the reader and require no theological annotation before they can convey the awe and drama of God's judging wrath.[16] Furthermore, their effectiveness as pieces of literature is matched by their importance at maintaining an essential ingredient in the witness of the Bible. That witness, to the judging work of God and his power to defeat evil and ultimately to root it out of the creation entirely, keeps the believing community from giving up its prophetic, sacrificial, and sometimes militant functions.

However, all of these same remarks could equally well be made about the important witnesses within Scripture to the intention of God to make good his promise to redeem the whole creation. The figure of Abraham setting out on a journey of faith, undergirded by an unconditional promise for himself, his progeny, and "all the families of the earth" (Gen. 12:1–9) is one example of an effective "working" text which points to God's plan for the salvation of the world. One can therefore speak of an *effective* diversity in Scripture which provides different themes with literary images so powerful as to have continued impact upon the lives of faith.

Thesis Two

Such effective diversity arises because the one Word to which the Scriptures witness is Incarnate. Christians confess that the entire canon of the Bible is a witness to Jesus Christ, the consummate Word of God. Such a perspective can be achieved only from a post-resurrection standpoint, and it is therefore not the perspective of every Biblical writer. However, from the Christian point of view, the unity within the Scriptures lies in the person and work of Jesus Christ. The motifs of judgment, reconciliation, and redemption, which achieve a normative expression in his life and resurrection, are motifs which run through the entire Scripture. The true character of the Scripture is also discernible in the Word made flesh. Just as the testimony to the nature and purpose of God is expressed in human and even veiled form in him, so too the Scriptures as a whole must be understood as incarnate words, words of faith about the subject and object of their faith. The Bible is "the witness without parallel" (Confession of 1967) to the Word, but it is a human and incarnate word in its own right. In a human and incarnate testimony, one must expect diversity, different points of view, conflict, and even contradiction. Passionate voices from many generations have spoken to the abiding motifs in the experience of the community of believers with God, and in so doing have given rise to the effective diversity of Scripture.

Thesis Three

No Biblical synthesis of these teachings is possible. They must be left as discrete themes, free to do their work; Biblical theology should be left free to present the ancient witness to the word of God in all the confusing, rich, and nuanced diversity in which it actually appears. At the same time, Christian Biblical theology has the task of discovering theological priorities within Scripture. The discussion in the previous sections of this chapter has already shown what peril we run if we attempt to reduce the diverse strands to a single "teaching of Scripture." No such synthesis is possible which does not do an injustice to one theme or another. The apocalyptic vision of the separation of the sheep and the goats in Matt. 25:31–46 and Paul's grand vision of cosmic redemption in I Cor. 15:20–28 simply cannot be synthesized. Indeed, we can be grateful that the Bible speaks to a motif such as divine retribution with so many voices. A less fully articulated Biblical literature on the subject might prove foreshortened and inadequate for our time or generations yet to come.

The first task of Biblical studies is to show the diversity of

Scripture. But the task cannot stop there. Interpreters need to take the next step of discerning the theological priorities within Scripture. This is done by simply raising the question "Is concept A more important than concept B to the large picture of the human dilemma and God's response which the Bible is painting?" A few people will resist such a question at an ideological level because they do not even admit that a variety of perspectives exists in Scripture. Others will resist the question on the grounds that there is no objective way to measure the relative "importance" of Biblical concepts and motifs. Yet, I submit that we do in fact assume the possibility of developing indigenous theological priorities within Scripture everytime we answer a searcher's question. "Do you want to know what the Bible teaches about divine punishment and retaliation? All right, I will give you several answers, all of which are Biblical teachings, but all of which are saying different things. . . . Which is the right answer, for you, in your dilemma today? That decision we will have to work out in the light of the entire sweep of the Biblical witness, and particularly in the light of the Word at the center of the Scripture!"

This thesis is really only another way of restating the ancient rule of interpretation, "Scripture is its own interpreter." Any Biblical motif or text should be interpreted with reference to the large context in which it stands, even if that context be as large as the entire canon.[17] This means it will always have to be interpreted in relation to other texts and themes which may run in quite a different direction. But the goal in the approach which I am outlining is ultimately not to suppress one Scripture with another Scripture, nor to cause all of them to appear to be saying the same thing. No, interpreting Scripture with Scripture, as I understand it, is to highlight the importance of particular texts and teachings by relating them to certain kerygmatic centers, and especially the Christological center of Scripture, while continuing to acknowledge variant witnesses even if they must be understood to command a lower level of priority. Only in some such way can sense be made out of the welter of divine Scriptural addresses to the same motifs.

Diversity can and must remain, but the Bible invites the interpreter to organize the Biblical data around those high-priority ideas, those kerygmatic centers, which are intrinsic to the text itself. Such an approach differs from that either of the literalist or the freewheeling impressionist. It will not suppress divergent themes of Scripture in favor of an organizing principle which the interpreter (instructed by a credo as much as by exegesis) insists on calling "the Biblical view."

Thesis Four

The confessions of the church can never present "the system of doctrine taught in Holy Scripture." Rather, their task is to present the faith in a manner comprehensible to their own time. As epitomes of the faith they must organize themselves around the theological priorities of their own time. Confessions (rather than the Scripture) are therefore ephemeral. For many years people were misled by the rhetoric of the church into thinking that the confessions were simply tightly organized summaries of Scripture. The fact is that confessions function above all to answer critics, to respond to the challenges of their own eras, and to organize doctrine in such a way that it can bring the received faith to bear upon the burning concerns of the day.

For this reason, confessions necessarily outlive their usefulness and have to be rewritten in every generation. These same remarks apply in varying measure to larger dogmatic treatises and systematic theologies, as well; however, the point is better illustrated by the more manageable brief statements. The United Presbyterian Church was right when, in 1967, it adopted an entire book of confessions culminating in one that has obsolescence built into its very title, "The Confession of 1967." As new crises arise the church attempts fresh formulations and alternative perspectives on the faith once delivered to the saints, to meet the new challenges.

The modern church has become increasingly aware that "a canon within the canon" is at work whenever a creed is written. The criteria used to discover that "canon within the canon" may not be Biblical at all, but cultural, political, and sociological in nature. A "canon within the canon" is not only necessary for a particular generation, it is inevitable. But it is also subject to change. By making the confession documents designed for limited normativeness, the church properly recognizes that any particular dogmatic statement, though often exceedingly definitive of the faith of its own time and place, and forever after a milestone along the way of the pilgrimage, will eventually need to be replaced. Only the Bible remains irreplacable and peerless. By making these clarifications the church may help the confessing community break out of the *a priori* biases established by the confessions by coming to the Scripture, upon whose authority alone it claims ultimately to stand.

This brings me to the most complex part of this discussion of the relationship of Biblical theology to dogmatic theology. Having just asserted that, in contrast to the Scriptures, dogmatic definitions large and small tend to outlive their usefulness, I would now argue that in the mediation of the truth of the Christian faith to any particular generation Biblical theology must work as the handmaiden to dogmatic theology. Confessions must necessarily be organized around the themes dictated by the experience of the church in the generations in which they are written. If our experience has been overshadowed by the specter of totalitarianism, then we may, as the writers of the Barmen Declaration did, be required to write our confession around the theme of obedience to the higher authority of God. Whether that particular theme is paramount in Scripture is in a sense irrelevant. Certainly it is a powerful theme of Scripture, and adequate to organize the convictions of a generation who are being pulled away into disobedience by the power of the state. Biblical data and motifs are available to those who would make sense of the dilemma of the believer in a particular generation. They can guide those writers into authentic affirmations of the Christian faith. But the starting point and the outline of their affirmation may be fundamentally their own.

On the other hand, there must be some authentic relationship between the central priorities of Scripture and those of the confessions. As I have shown earlier, the task of Biblical theology is not to reduce all the Biblical witness to a set of homogenized themes. Rather, it must allow the Scripture to stand clear in its multiplicity of ideas, while at the same time identifying priorities intrinsic to the Scriptures themselves. Von Rad can write an *Old Testament Theology* in which *Heilsgeschichte* is the central priority and the traditioning process itself becomes an organizing principle.[18] Eichrodt, on the other hand, can make covenant the top priority in the first volume of his *Theology of the Old Testament.* He does this not because he necessarily brought to the text any conviction that it should be so, but because in his best judgment covenant is in fact the central organizing principle of the Pentateuch.[19] If we really can discover central theological affirmations in the Scripture, it seems highly probable that contemporary theological expressions will build upon the structure intrinsic to the theology of the Bible itself. Although the final, agreed-upon account of the order of priorities within the Biblical tradition as a whole has yet to be written down, Biblical and systematic theologians alike can agree at least upon the most important kerygmatic center of all, that is, the Christological confession. Even to spell out that theme in detail is, as we all know, extremely complex. However, any attempt to make Christian sense of the witness of the Scripture on any theological issue has constantly to return to this central facet of Biblical affirmation.

What shall we say, then, about the relationship of Scrip-

tural priorities to those of theology? I see a dialectical movement between the two. If my concern as a layperson, pastor,
or professional theologian is to speak to the human propensity to interpret suffering as punishment and to attribute
death and destruction to the judging activity of God, I will
on the one hand want to start building my case upon the
specific contours which the problem has assumed in my own
time. Auschwitz will add a contour; the H-bomb will add a
contour; insights of psychiatry will add a contour. This structure will give the basic shape to my address to the problem.
But I will also want to turn to Scripture to examine its treatment of the matter. While allowing Scripture to interpret
Scripture (which is not allowing one text to cancel out another, but rather asking how the diversity and even conflict
within the Bible itself can correct and enrich my understanding of any particular text), ultimately I will have to build out
toward the contemporary problem from one relevant strand
of Scriptural development or another. If, in the case of the
motif of divine retribution, I choose to build upon that strand
in the Scripture which depicts God ultimately as the redeemer rather than the wrathful judge, I cannot reject that
second strand. I have simply to demonstrate that for the
Bible itself the priority lies with the redemption motif. As the
nuanced Biblical theological interpretation of the motif of
divine retribution is built into the systematic development of
the problem, the two sets of priorities meet and are joined.
If they differ in their order, a decision must be made whether
to reconcile them or allow them to remain in some acknowledged tension.

   This discussion leads me to a final point under my fourth
thesis. It may not really be possible to talk directly about
"Biblical perspectives on current issues." The Bible really
cannot properly speak to current issues without first becoming related to a systematic theological perspective on the
issues. The Bible is a handmaiden to that theological perspec-

tive. The latter, however, can only be faithful if it respects not only the data but in some way the priorities within the Bible itself.[20]

Thesis Five

Appropriate Christian theological priorities for our time include the themes of reconciliation and redemption. Confessions organized around such motifs will understand the motif of divine retribution as supportive of and comprehended by the purposes of divine reconciliation and redemption. The United Presbyterian Confession of 1967 and the Proposed Confession of the Presbyterian Church in the U.S. acknowledge the diversity of Scriptural ways of speaking about God's judgment and retribution. They also acknowledge and ultimately build primarily upon themes other than judgment and retribution in dealing with the hope of the believer. The Confession of 1967, as is well known, is organized around the theme of reconciliation. God's righteous wrath and judging role are acknowledged. But wrath and love are brought into close juxtaposition, as in 9.14: "God's love never changes. Against all who oppose him, God expresses his love in wrath. In the same love God took upon himself judgment and shameful death in Jesus Christ, to bring men to repentance and new life." The Confession, while building upon Biblical themes, does not necessarily present them in the same order of importance, by any quantitative measurement at least, in which they are presented in the Bible. The organizing priority is set by the crisis and the need of the Christian community in 1967. For that community, the possibility of reconciliation in Jesus Christ—itself certainly a central Biblical priority—provides an interpretive principle that can erect a structure into which the theological data of the Bible can be built. In the process, the quantitatively massive Biblical witness to the motif of divine retribution is not allowed to build up that theme beyond at most a parity relationship to the motif of divine redemption.

Ultimate divine judgment is defined only once in the Confession of 1967: "To receive life from the risen Lord is to have life eternal; to refuse life from him is to choose death which is separation from God" (9.11). This definition appears to build upon the possibility, known mostly by inverse implication from passages which speak of eternal life as God's gift through the Christ (Col. 3:3–4; James 1:12), that some Biblical thinking about The Retribution could conceive of eschatological punishment as simply the deprivation of continued life in the presence of God.[21] It does not specifically reject those other strands, which describe God's judgment as being cast into outer darkness (Matt. 25:30) or eternal punishment in the lake of fire (Rev. 20:15). In a fuller treatment, of course, such strands would be recognized as part of the multiplex Scriptural witness to the matter; however, the Confession quite properly has built toward the Scripture from priorities which substantially reduce the importance of such Biblical language. Quite properly, I say, because in the full context of the canonical witness to the motifs of retribution and redemption such language proves to be of secondary importance in the Biblical tradition itself.

The subordination of the motif of divine retribution to that of redemption in the Confession of 1967 becomes most evident in the final chapter, "The Fulfillment of Reconciliation." This is the chapter dealing with eschatology. Here the contrast with the Westminster Confession is perhaps most stark.

> Biblical visions and images of the rule of Christ such as a heavenly city, a father's house, a new heaven and earth, a marriage feast, and an unending day culminate in the image of the kingdom. The kingdom represents the triumph of God over all that resists his will and disrupts his creation. Already God's reign is present as a ferment in the world, stirring hope in men and preparing the world to receive its ultimate judgment and redemption. (9.54)
>
> With an urgency born of this hope the church applies itself to

present tasks and strives for a better world. It does not identify limited progress with the kingdom of God on earth, nor does it despair in the face of disappointment and defeat. In steadfast hope the church looks beyond all partial achievement to the final triumph of God. (9.55)

"The kingdom" is, for the Confession of 1967, the culminating eschatological image. As this section reveals, "the kingdom" is understood in terms of theodicy. "The kingdom" is the product of God's ultimate vindication of his way of dealing with his rebellious creation. "The kingdom" is his triumph. What the Confession says about judgment is minimal; about damnation it here says nothing more than that all evil shall be "banished from his creation" (9.53). Earlier in the Confession the theme of redemption is placed at least on a par with the theme of judgment; now, a disparity in favor of the redemption motif emerges. In the concluding chapters of this book I will argue that this disparity is more faithful to the priorities within the Scripture (as revealed in its literary architecture as well as its specific teachings) than was the old Westminster imparity in favor of "retribution."

Unfortunately it is not possible to make any statement at this writing about the Proposed Confession of the Presbyterian Church in the U.S., inasmuch as the final text of the document is still being worked out. The preliminary document, however, reveals a decision similar to that of the drafters of the Confession of 1967 to reduce the impact within the Confession of the motif of divine retribution, again in line with better Scriptural understanding and more urgent contemporary theological priorities. The study notes identify X.4 as the section dealing with "heaven and hell, ultimate salvation and damnation."[22] And yet neither "heaven," "hell," nor "damnation" is used in the section. We are said to live "in tension between God's warnings and promises." The text continues, "Knowing the righteous judgment of God in Christ, we urge all people to be reconciled to God, not exempting ourselves from the warnings. Constrained by

God's love in Christ, we have good hope for all people, not exempting the most unlikely from the promises. Judgment belongs to God and not to us. We are confident that God's future for every person will be both merciful and just" (X.4, lines 62–71).

WHERE TO BEGIN

How will this exercise proceed if we take seriously the principles outlined above? We will have to begin by confessing that the resurrection of Jesus Christ stands at the center of the entire witness of the canon to God's judging activity. But if Christ's act upon the cross and his Easter victory are done once and for all on behalf of all persons dead, living, and yet unborn, then we will have to affirm with Brunner that the Word of God Incarnate is a word which leads and challenges people to say "yes," not "no," to God's perfecting purpose. The evangelical word comes with a single purpose, that of redemption, and not the dual purpose of redemption and condemnation.[23] The divine program of redemption stresses the goodness of the world, the importance of human beings in their individuality, the continuity of flesh and spirit, and the resurrection of every individual in a spiritual body. The Bible is an account of the overcoming of this body of death by a body of life, an account of the undoing of the Fall, and the return to a state of immediacy between creation and Creator. It is within the large context of this account that the Biblical treatments of God's way with evil, his retributive justice, and his actions of cursing and blessing, rewarding and punishing should be understood.

A Summary

This is the midpoint of this study. Before moving on, we need to review the steps taken so far. I began with brief narratives illustrative of the forms which the religious fear of retribution takes when it contributes to personal spiritual and intellectual crises. Because it contributes so substantially to so many pastoral problems, I have argued from the beginning that the motif of divine retribution is a burning contemporary issue.

But the motif of divine retribution is also a Biblical issue. Chapter II was therefore devoted to brief exegetical treatments of six representative texts, ranging from the earliest to the latest phases of Biblical writing. All of them in one way or another present God as one who metes out his justice retributively, responding to evil with curse, punishment, and even damnation, and to good, with blessing. In reviewing these texts and some of the discussion of the commentators, we discovered numerous leads within the retributional texts themselves toward ways of understanding these texts which would overcome their most programmatic and rigid implications. One of these leads examined in some detail was the hypothesis of K. Koch. Based upon a dynamistic understanding of language in ancient Israel, deeds were thought to be in themselves "destiny-producing." In this view, which I regard as provocative but mostly nondemonstrable, evil unleashes its own consequences; God's role is simply providential.

In turning to eschatological and apocalyptic literature of the Old and New Testaments, I supported the thesis that apocalyptic is simply heightened and imaginative eschatology in which the themes of conflict, judgment, and restoration have become cosmic in scope. This view of the nature of apocalyptic literature led to the thesis that "as a detailed account of factual matters regarding the future of the universe, the apocalyptic scenario is of no value." The validity of that thesis at a simple textual level was borne out when I attempted to reconstruct the sequence of The Retribution from Rev., ch. 20. If the details of the apocalyptic scenario are of no predictive value, the question becomes, "What then is the value of apocalyptic, and what kerygma lies behind the colorful facade of the language of cosmic catastrophe and judgment?" My answer to this question remains as yet fully to be stated; however, it is clear that part of the message of this material is the assertion of the seriousness of God's anger and judgment against evil. Divine retribution is thus an undoubted element in the witness of Daniel and the Apocalypse of John. But other elements in the kerygma include a teleological understanding of history, with the future culminating in a perfected universe brought about by God's redemptive activity.

In Chapter III, I surveyed two of the older confessional statements regarding the matter of divine retribution, and discovered therein a failure to recognize the full diversity in the Biblical data on the motif. After pointing to the great diversity of Scriptural witness on matters having to do with God's treatment of good and evil, and finding no evident key to harmonizing all of these, I argued that the task of Biblical theology is to discover priorities intrinsic to Scripture itself according to which one theme may legitimately be set over others in order of importance. A proper interpretation of the ongoing motif of divine retribution must set it in relation to the Christological center of the Bible and in relation to the redemption motif so strongly identified with that center. The assertion of this relationship of the redemption motif to the retribution motif makes clear the next stage to which this study should move. It now becomes my task to cycle once again through the Bible, following the motif of the divine purpose of redemption through a number of texts. In this way alone can I support the thesis that the motif of divine redemption does not merely countervail the motif of divine retribution, but actually encompasses and comprehends it.

Chapter IV

THE DIVINE "YES" AS CONTEXT FOR THE DIVINE "NO"

The divine "yes" refers to those texts within the Old and New Testaments which highlight and develop the ongoing Biblical motif of God's redeeming purpose. In the pages that follow, I repeat the pattern which I used in Chapter II in dealing with a series of passages from the Pentateuch, prophets, wisdom tradition of the Old Testament; and gospel, epistle, and apocalyptic materials from the New Testament. First, the Revised Standard Version of the text is printed. Then, I give a brief exegesis of the passage and a review of the scholarly literature on it under the heading "Discussion." Finally, by means of some paragraphs on "Direction," I attempt to show the relationship of the passage to the developing outline of the motif of God's redeeming purpose.

THE WORLD AS A THEATER OF REDEMPTION

Text

14 The LORD God said to the serpent, "Because you have done this, cursed are you above all cattle, and above all wild animals; upon your belly you shall go, and dust you shall eat all the days of your life. 15 I will put enmity between you and the woman, and between your seed and her seed; he shall bruise your head, and you shall bruise his heel." 16 To the woman he said, "I will greatly multiply your pain in childbear-

ing; in pain you shall bring forth children, yet your desire shall be for your husband, and he shall rule over you." 17 And to Adam he said, "Because you have listened to the voice of your wife, and have eaten of the tree of which I commanded you, 'You shall not eat of it,' cursed is the ground because of you; in toil you shall eat of it all the days of your life; 18 thorns and thistles it shall bring forth to you; and you shall eat the plants of the field. 19 In the sweat of your face you shall eat bread till you return to the ground, for out of it you were taken; you are dust, and to dust you shall return."

20 The man called his wife's name Eve, because she was the mother of all living. 21 And the LORD God made for Adam and for his wife garments of skins, and clothed them.

22 Then the LORD God said, "Behold, the man has become like one of us, knowing good and evil; and now, lest he put forth his hand and take also of the tree of life, and eat, and live for ever"—23 therefore the LORD God sent him forth from the garden of Eden, to till the ground from which he was taken. 24 He drove out the man; and at the east of the garden of Eden he placed the cherubim, and a flaming sword which turned every way, to guard the way to the tree of life.

—Genesis 3:14–24

Discussion

Before there can be a drama of salvation, there must be a need for it. That is why I have chosen to begin the discussion of the great Biblical redemption motif with the curse laid after the Fall upon the serpent, Adam, and Eve. This decision is not entirely arbitrary because it follows Israel's own sense of direction in attaching the creation stories to the Pentateuch.

It may be useful to review the redactional history of the Pentateuch and comment on the effect of the redaction upon the originally separate myths, legends, and historical accounts which are brought together by the process. Scholars are now widely agreed that the primeval history of Gen., chs.

1 to 11, was attached to the saga of the patriarchs and the history of Israel only at the last stage of the development of the earliest source of the Pentateuch.[1] Taking a cycle of myths about creation that were Israel's version of the common stock in the ancient Near East, some religious genius[2] or geniuses at the court of David or Solomon who put in writing the first great account of Israel's beginnings worked back from history toward prehistory. What the Yahwist source says about the creative work of God was affected by what the writer(s) already knew his providential and historical work to have been. The Yahweh whose name Israel had already learned through Moses' experience at the burning bush, whose power Israel had witnessed in the exodus event, whose will Israel had come to know at Sinai, was now recognized as the Creator of the whole world. Obviously, such a linkage of the once independent primeval history to the history of Israel was bound to have a profound effect upon the significance of the mythic tradition. In fact, it substantially overcame the original function of these stories which, like myth everywhere, was to help the culture account for the perceived realities of the world. It sought to answer those who want to know why the sky is blue, why human sexuality exists, why women suffer in childbirth, and why men have to sweat to wrest bread from the soil. In the new redactional setting the accounts now become theology writing.[3] The Fall and all that follows through Gen., ch. 11, now inaugurate a great theological drama of salvation which begins with Abraham and stretches down to the writer's own time.

The immediate text at hand reflects the keen interest of the J source in maintaining some of the earlier mythic stress on human questions of why things are as they are. Here are found implicit or explicit accounts of the origin of human fear of snakes, the subordination of the wife to the husband, sin, work, and clothing. Evidently the curse upon the serpent (3:14–15) is intended among other things to account for that creature's peculiar mode of locomotion. But the new setting for this passage within the prologue to the great drama of redemption renders this explanation, like the rest of the details of the curse, substantially immaterial. Whether the serpent actually got around in some other way prior to the curse is utterly irrelevant now, in spite of the fact that William Jennings Bryan did not acknowledge it to be so at the Scopes trial.[4] The serpent's fate is now part of a theological judgment that the created world shares in the separated, broken, and cursed relationship which derives from human disobedience and which continues to characterize life in the world.

The broken relationship with the Creator is also revealed in the accursed pain of childbirth (3:16) and in the sweating of the workman (vs. 17–19). Verse 19b seems to be not so much a curse as a statement of fact: "You are dust, and to dust you shall return." It is a reprise back to the story of the creation of man in Gen. 2:7; however, it too contrasts the mortality of the man in the order which is now beginning with the blessed possibility of immortality, now lost forever (vs. 22–23).

Or is it lost forever? In v. 24 the writer seems to intend to leave Eden intact in some mysterious unknown eastern place, still available for occupancy, should the curse somehow be overcome.

Direction

Can we get back to the garden, back to the unity, simplicity, and peace of the pre-cursed state? Today the question is a fiercely burning one. It may be asked more passionately in our own generation than it has been for many years. As a realist and an heir of the Calvinistic tradition, my instinctive answer is, "No way!" Not short of the Eschaton will women find themselves in a pre-cursed state in which they do not have to deal with the domination of their husbands and when childbearing is not painful. Serpents will continue to crawl on their bellies, men will continue to earn their bread by the sweat of their brows, and people will die. Although Christians testify that by taking their stand in Christ they are justified, sanctified, and the burden of sin is removed, like everyone else Christians suffer pain in childbirth, sweat as they till their fields, and finally die. As modern individuals we have to affirm that there was never a time when these things were untrue, for the world of living creatures knows no other possibilities. In other words, the details of Gen. 3:14–24 are wrong, for they do not give an actual account of the beginnings of these human sorrows. But set in their theological context, they do bring us a crucially important message. That message is this: Somewhere a garden exists whose occupants could enjoy a pristine relationship with God. The writer of Gen. 3:24 may have meant it literally; we can understand it only metaphorically, as a brilliant image of a lost but not utterly vanquished possibility of a pristine relationship between human beings and God. That powerful image of the empty garden with the closely guarded gate is adequate to set in motion the great Biblical drama of redemption.

If this analysis of the result of placing the creation stories at the head of the history of God's peoples is correct, then for the Biblical narrative the world truly does become a theater of redemption. Driven on by the powerful effect of the image of a lost paradise, which causes generation after generation to say, "we got to get ourselves back to the garden,"[5] the entire Biblical story, in broad outline, can be interpreted as an account of God's leading and man's tortuous following along on the road back to Eden.[6] It is a drama of promise and fulfillment, in which the fulfillment reverts again to promise. The scheme is objectively observable in Scripture and has often been pointed out.[7] The goal of a repristinization of the human relationship with God is sometimes stated explicitly and sometimes simply evoked with such images as the land flowing with milk and honey, new heaven and new earth, river of life, highway of our God, New Jerusalem, Kingdom of Heaven on earth, and Torah written upon the heart.

Into what sequence does this drama of redemption fall? It

has a prologue and four acts. The creation stories, the prologue, have the function of setting over against human history (which everybody since the J writer has understood to be alienated, fragmented, and sinful) a picture of what might have been. They tell of the Fall, and give the faintest hint of what might yet be. The prologue has the function of placing Israel and her fellow pilgrim, the church, at the very center of the effort to recover that lost pristine relationship with God. In Gen. 12:1–4 the fate of all humanity's deep desire to overcome the curse of Babel and indeed all the curses of the past hangs upon the obedience of one man.[8] That man is the progenitor of Israel; and it is through the faithfulness of Israel and that of its offspring, the church, that God, in his own time and way, will move the entire world back toward the garden.

Act I is the period from the promise to Abraham of the land flowing with milk and honey to the fulfillment of that promise by the end of the Book of Joshua. Act II recounts the failure of that fulfillment, visible in various ways from the beginning of the monarchy down to the end of the Old Testament. But it is also the stage in which the prophets, the Deuteronomic historians, and the eschatological writers lift up a new promise, the promise of survival, restoration, and ultimate vindication. Act III can be described as a reinterpretation of that promise in a new fulfillment, given in the Gospel account of the coming of the Messiah. The final act has the least extensive literary representation in the Bible, and yet it has had a powerful influence over the history of Christian experience ever since. I refer to New Testament eschatology, and to the encouragement which it gives to God's people to work and struggle toward the New Jerusalem which will be manifested fully at the Parousia. It is my contention that this entire Biblical drama in four acts is concerned with a quest to recover the right relationship with God which existed in pristine form in Eden. The world is the theater in which that drama is played out and the sought redemption is already substantially assured before the Biblical portion of the drama ends. If this is a correct analysis, we are looking at a "Scriptural priority" when we look at this drama of redemption. In fact, the history of salvation can be regarded as the single most encompassing framework of Scripture, into which all other themes of Scripture are crafted.

How does this drama of redemption leading toward the goal of the recovery of an innocent and right relationship of mankind with God relate to the claim which the church has always identified as the "highest priority" in Scripture, namely, the Christological assertion? How can it all be seen *sub specie Christi?* In his *Creation and Fall,* Dietrich Bonhoeffer brilliantly explored this question through the typological relationship of the old Adam to the new Adam.[9] Bonhoeffer invoked the tree in the garden as the limitation on the possibilities of mankind, a horizon beyond which the first couple could not move to view the purposes and will of God. The man and woman spoiled their pristine relationship by seeking to extend their horizons beyond that limit.[10] For a long time mankind groped toward reestablishing a right relationship with God until at last a new limit was erected in a new garden, namely, the cross on Golgotha. At the cross, men once again confront the limit beyond which they cannot press to know the hiddenness of God. And yet by accepting this new limit of the cross, something much closer to a pristine relationship can be found: a reopening of the door of hope. Bonhoeffer's treatment thus ties both the Fall at the beginning of the drama and the restoration at the end of it to the Cross in the middle. The movement of the whole is toward the restoration of the full relationship enjoyed in the innocence of the garden.

One question remains: Who will walk through the gates of the new Eden at the last day to take their places around the throne of the Lamb? The prologue of the drama of redemption does not make this clear. This much, however, I would point out: The scope of the redemption motif is from its outset universal. The prologue of the drama involves the world as a whole; it is the creation as a whole which falls in Adam's sin and now groans for its redemption. The promise to Abraham is that through his fidelity all the nations, not just Israel, can come back together again. The act at the center of the drama is done once, for all. No doubt God wills that the whole creation return to conformity with the basic goodness in which he created it in the beginning. No doubt his history is moving that way. And yet the new Eden is a matured and perfected paradise, a New Jerusalem more cosmopolitan, more brilliant than the first. How is it to be matured and perfected? Through long experience, through the suffering of history? Through wrath? Can full redemption be achieved only through divine retribution? Will only those who can walk past the flaming sword enter the gates of the New Jerusalem? Or have the ultimate wrath and punishment already been satisfied by the sacrifice of the Lamb of God upon the cross, so that all creatures can hope for a share in the world to come?

PROPHETIC PROMISE

Text

> 8 How can I give you up, O Ephraim! How can I hand you over, O Israel! How can I make you like Admah! How can I treat you like Zeboiim! My heart recoils within me, my compassion grows warm and tender. 9 I will not execute my fierce anger, I will not again destroy Ephraim; for I am God and not man, the Holy One in your midst, and I will not come to destroy.
>
> —*Hosea 11:8–9*

Discussion

On our earlier cycle through the text of the Old Testament, we examined Hos. 4:1–3, a clear-cut prophetic threat of doom and judgment.[11] In that passage, God was proclaimed to be the retributor and judge who would extirpate evil from his land. In ch. 11, on the other hand, a series of oracles which defy the usual formal descriptions are to be found. They resemble nothing so much as Jeremiah's confessions or oracles of lament,[12] except that here it is not the prophet but Yahweh himself who sighs at the tragedy of his people. The oracle presents God's own mind alternating between curse and blessing, judgment and hope. Inasmuch as vs. 8–9 are clearly promissory in nature, one is left with the impression that God is rejecting his decision to destroy and deciding instead to redeem his people from exile and trouble.

A closer inspection of the passage confirms this impression. Verse 8 anticipates the language of Deut. 29:23 (29:22 Hebrew) with its threats against Admah and Zeboiim. And yet, as compared to the threats of Deuteronomy, the word of Yahweh here is a word of anguish and unresolved tension. In the former, God has no choice but to punish, for the covenant formulation of the law requires that the curse be implemented against those who disobey. Through Hosea, Yahweh expresses compassion at the fate of his people. Precisely because Yahweh is God and not man, the holy one in Israel's midst, can he come not to destroy but to redeem his people? The Hebrew word *'āshūb,* translated in the RSV, "I will . . . again," is a key word in assessing the precise date (and therefore authorship) of this passage. If the word is correct as it stands and is correctly rendered in this way, the writer would either have had to have known a destruction of Ephraim, the northern Israelite kingdom, prior to its final dissolution as a political entity in 722/1 B.C. by Sargon II,[13] or else he is referring to the final destruction of 722/1 itself. If the former is the case, the author of the oracle could have been Hosea himself; if the latter is the point of reference, the writer could not have been Hosea. We will return to this issue subsequently.

The text, in the last analysis, is a prophetic oracle of promise. Therefore it is an example of the prophetic development of that redemption motif which was already well established in the J writer's narrative framework for Pentateuchal theology and history. The drama of redemption is forwarded here when God rejects the demands of his own law and justice in order to take compassion upon his wayward people.

Although I am using this Hosea promise oracle as representative of the relatively limited number of oracles of promise in the eighth-century prophets, I should like briefly to depart from my usual pattern of using only one such illustrative text to examine another. Amos 9:11–15 is the only oracle of promise in that otherwise entirely threatening prophetic book. For that reason, it has often been thought to be a later addition to the work of Amos. The oracle begins with Yahweh's promise that "in that day I will raise up the booth of David that is fallen," and goes on to picture the Israel of the future as a nation which enjoys prosperity and security in a fertile land. As in Hosea, the language of the Amos passage appears to be in some kind of dialogue with the curse-and-blessing scheme of Deut., chs. 27 to 29. The very blessings which Deuteronomy enumerates and then threatens to destroy should the curse be pronounced are the content of this passage—sweet wine, rebuilt cities, vineyards and gardens and fruit. One might account for this fact by arguing that Amos and the northern prophetic circles surrounding him had not yet abandoned hope that the retributive, judging action of God can ultimately be transcended through the compassionate action of God. Or one could argue that the passage is the work of a later age which had known the destruction of 722/1 and possibly even that of 587 B.C., but, because the destruction was not total, had begun again to see a ray of hope. Does it stem from a later age which, because of such experience, had rejected the idea that God would so fully implement his retributive curse that no possibility of further survival could remain?

Questions of the date and the authorship of the oracles of promise in the early classical prophets have occupied scholars for many years. I pause over the matter here because of what is at stake for my thesis. If the oracles represent an element of hope held by the eighth-century prophets or their immediate circles, then the dialectic between the retributional and redemptionist motifs is early and deeply rooted in the Old Testament prophetic tradition. It may even be in some kind of continuity with the positive drama of salvation begun in the earliest Pentateuchal source. Then it could truly be said that in no stratum of the Bible is the theme of God's judgment sounded without the contrapuntal theme of God's mercy being sounded as well. On the other hand, if the promise oracles are added to the early prophets by a later revisionist, one would have to recognize the work of these prophets as the unmitigated proclamation of divine wrath and retribution.

Scholarly discussion of the matter can be well illustrated by contrasting the positions of J. Philip Hyatt and William F. Stinespring. Hyatt was one of those who defended the "authenticity of the prophetic oracles of hope." For Hyatt there is a tension of grace and judgment running throughout the prophetic canon and this is especially visible in Hosea. In the old but still useful work *Prophetic Religion*,[14] he gives to the passage that we have been examining the superscription, "The nature of God must include mercy and love as well as strict justice." His translation of the passage reveals his understanding of the key word in v. 9: "I will not execute my fierce anger! I will not turn *('āshūb)* to destroy Ephraim!" This translation avoids the question of whether the author knew of a destruction of the Northern Kingdom by selecting a different semantical option for the rendition of the word, but it also maintains the lively possibility that it is from Hosea's own lips.

W. F. Stinespring replied to Hyatt's work in an article entitled "Hosea, Prophet of Doom."[15] After showing that vs. 8 and 9 belong together, Stinespring argues that "both verses together constitute a post-Hoseanic interpolation by a hope editor."[16] In large part, he bases the argument on the contention that *ʾashūb* in v. 9 must mean "again" and therefore implies a prior destruction of the Northern Kingdom. In the light of similar judgments regarding other Hoseanic oracles of hope, Stinespring concludes that Hosea is as much a prophet of doom as Amos, Isaiah, Micah, and even Jeremiah, and that there is no inkling in any of these writers of a romantic wavering on Yahweh's part between vengeance and compassion.

If the position represented by Stinespring can be validated, one would want to ask why a later redactor of hope would incorporate into the purely judgmental traditions of the older prophetic canon a vision of divine reward and blessing. One reason for such an editorial process would have been to correct the apparent error made by the earlier prophets in foretelling a total and utter obliteration of Israel, thus saving their credibility. A second would arise from the fact that in the later development of the prophetic tradition in Ezekiel and II Isaiah, the prognosis of hope became a legitimate and major prophetic theme. But what about the authority of these "spurious" additions in the eighth-century prophets? Would it not be seriously flawed?

An interesting modulation of scholarly language has taken place since the debates regarding the "authenticity" of the oracles of promise in the older prophets were at their peak in the '40s and '50s. Scholars seem to be more and more reluctant to use words like "genuine," "authentic," and "spurious." Many no longer consider a text to be lacking in authority simply because it happens to come from a mouth other than that of the figure whose name stands at the beginning of the book in which it appears. In the context of the whole canon, the question of whether a particular passage is from exactly the same chronological horizon and literary hand as that to which it is attached becomes much less significant. As long as the appended oracle bears comparison with kerygmatic centers of the Biblical tradition, it can be regarded as of authoritative importance even in a nonoriginal context. The tracing of redactional history can show how the theological themes of the Bible grow in the face of historical events. In this way it is possible to watch the faith correcting a too heavy emphasis by the addition of modifying or even opposing teachings. In short, we have come full circle. First higher criticism created a furor by discerning different authors within Biblical works. Then criticism tended to reject those portions of Biblical books which appeared to be additions to the work of the original authors, regarding them simply as glosses. Now scholarship and theology alike are again trying to view all texts within the larger context of the canon in a serious effort to validate their authority wherever possible. This new situation has arisen partly because the critical proofs of the exact authorship of particular passages often have not been satisfying or even demonstrable, and partly because people have continued to discover literary and theological values in texts which were formerly dismissed as "spurious" additions.[17]

The issue of the date and authorship of the promise oracles in the earlier prophets can be solved in three ways with two results as far as the issues of this book are concerned. One can reject the promise oracles as "mere" late additions, with the result that the weight of the prophetic canon leans more substantially toward the motif of divine retribution. One can accept the promise oracles as the work of the prophets in question or their immediate circles, in which case the two motifs of retribution and redemption continue to interact and correct one another within the early prophetic canon.

Or one can argue that the oracles of promise in Hosea and Amos were deliberately inserted at a point when subsequent Old Testament thought saw it necessary to right the balance away from an overweening emphasis on divine judgment, in which case the two motifs would appear to be moving toward an overall parity.

The prophetic oracles of promise pointed to a time of restoration at some future stage of God's activity. By the time of Deutero-Isaiah, the time of restoration was clearly near at hand. Beginning with 538 B.C., a program of restoration based upon these hopes was set into motion. The writer of Isa., chs. 56 to 66, living during or after this program of restoration, could also recognize that this fulfillment is not all that the prophetic vision had foreseen. Were the prophets of hope, therefore, as inaccurate as the prophets of doom? Was the promise of restoration by God to be as imperfectly fulfilled as the threat of divine destruction? Little by little postexilic Israel saw the imagery of prophetic hope as incapable of fulfillment in any literal way short of a divine intervention and alteration of the creation as it was known. Gradually the tradition of promise moved toward the apocalyptic vision. That tradition also provided the basis upon which the early Christians could interpret their experience with the risen Lord. The Christ was for them the fulfillment of the prophetic oracles of hope, although the fulfillment radically reinterpreted the promise.

Direction

Does the debate over the authenticity of the early prophetic oracles of promise and whether the same prophetic teachers could have dealt at the same time in the motifs of divine retribution and divine redemption mean that we should not take these oracles seriously? Certainly not. Whoever its author may have been—and in the balance I would side with those who consider it one of Hosea's own teachings —Hos. 11:8–9 is a devoted, profoundly honest, and moving insight into the dilemma of God in dealing with his fractious people. As such, it and the other promise oracles of which it is merely illustrative must be tested against the center of the canon as well as seen within its overall framework. When viewed in relation to these norms, I believe the prophetic oracles of promise emerge as authentic witnesses to the saving and redeeming work of God. They may not be accurate in all details, nor correct in their time frame. But certainly their message that God's plan to overcome the evil of this world will be vindicated precisely in the redemption and restoration of his people squares with the Word of God to whom all the Scriptures witness. Ultimately the prophetic oracles of promise have their own vindication in the Christ in whom appeared the compassion (Hos. 11:8–9), and the beginning of a new and secure world order (Amos 9:11–15), which they foresaw.

The questions that have confronted us in both steps of this return trip through the Biblical text remain: Is the promise available only through fire? Is redemption possible only to individuals and a world which have suffered the pangs of divine retribution? Perhaps the prophetic canon as a whole can begin to shape an answer. When I look at that canon, intricately relating justice and mercy as it does all the way from the punishing God of Amos, ch. 8, to the rewarding God of Isa., ch. 65, the answer I get sounds very much like the words of a good father to his disobedient son or daughter: "If you insist on tempting fate and on disobeying, you will have to suffer the consequences. I will support those who inflict those consequences upon you, for it is only right and just that this should be done. You may have to go through hell! But I will also be here to try to help and to persuade and ultimately to provide a safe haven in which you can get it together again. And I will never, never let you down!"

UNCONVENTIONAL ANSWERS TO ANGUISH

Text

16 Moreover I saw under the sun that in the place of justice, even there was wickedness, and in the place of righteousness, even there was wickedness. 17 I said in my heart, God will judge the righteous and the wicked, for he has appointed a time for every matter, and for every work. 18 I said in my heart with regard to the sons of men that God is testing them to show them that they are but beasts. 19 For the fate of the sons of men and the fate of beasts is the same; as one dies, so dies the other. They all have the same breath, and man has no advantage over the beasts; for all is vanity. 20 All go to one place; all are from the dust, and all turn to dust again. 21 Who knows whether the spirit of man goes upward and the spirit of the beast goes down to the earth? 22 So I saw that there is nothing better than that a man should enjoy his work, for that is his lot; who can bring him to see what will be after him?

—*Ecclesiastes 3:16–22*

Discussion

In the two previous sections of this chapter, I have discussed Biblical texts which affirm the redemptive polarity of the Scripture over against its retributional opposite. In contrast to the *lex talionis* and the Deuteronomic *Heilsgeschichte* of reward-and-punishment, I set the Yahwist's affirmation of God's determination to lead mankind on the way back to Eden. Over against the prophetic oracles of judgment and divine retribution, I examined certain early prophetic oracles of the promise of restoration. With the wisdom tradition it is not so easily possible to discern contiguous examples of the two great contrasting Scriptural approaches to God's justice and his compassion. In the Psalter one finds no dialogue between the Psalms of the Two Ways and any psalm of God's one way. Outside the Psalter no wisdom texts extensively develop the theme of God's redemptive purpose.

In the wisdom tradition of the Old Testament, the contrast is more between the rigid and naive scheme of retribution contained in the Psalms of the Two Ways[18] and the acid rejection of that scheme in the books of Ecclesiastes and Job. Between these two literary collections there is no polite dialogue. On the contrary, the latter attack the edifice of the retribution scheme in the former with the aim of destroying it. Ecclesiastes leaves it in a shambles. Job begins to point beyond the ruin of the retribution scheme to some better understanding of God's way of dealing with the world, though no motif of renewal and redemption is fully developed.

I shall chart the outlines of this wisdom attack on the Old Testament motif of divine reward-and-punishment by brief studies in both Ecclesiastes and Job, beginning with the former. The book itself is frequently dated during the Persian period, at about the sixth century B.C. It is a unique book in the Old Testament in that it is essentially a rationalistic treatment of a theological question. In contrast to the pithy and oracular style of the prophetic books and the passionate nature even of other wisdom literature, the Preacher attacks the problem of God's sufferance of evil in the world in an almost philosophical manner. R. B. Y. Scott asserts that the thought of Ecclesiastes centers on four themes.[19] First, the writer asserts that life itself is an endless movement without change. Second, from the point of view of the Preacher, whatever happens in life appears to be predetermined, but the why of this predetermination is not known. Third, the theory that divine retribution inevitably overtakes wickedness and that goodness brings prosperity to the righteous is rejected out of hand as not conforming to experience. This even applies to any automatic cause-and-effect sequence in which destiny-producing deeds unleash their own chain of consequences. Fourth, all values in life are negated by their opposites, so that life is followed by death, excellence by misfortune, and happiness by sorrow.

Does Ecclesiastes then deny God's existence? No, but by focusing on God's transcendence and remoteness from the cause-and-effect sequence of human experience, the writer is struck dumb on the question of God's role in human experience. If one looks at God's all-powerful, all-just nature and then looks at the world in contrast, one can say nothing. The two simply do not match. The book thus shows the impossibility of trying to build a moral code or even an explanation of experience upon God's transcendent attributes. This does not mean that the Preacher is agnostic or atheistic; indeed, the gifts of life are from God (3:13). But a personal and intervening God who rewards and punishes according to established principles appears to be absent. The Preacher cannot follow the prophets in the conclusions which they draw either from God's justice or his mercy. Do you expect God's absolute justice to be manifested in events? Forget it! "There is a vanity which takes place on earth, that there are righteous men to whom it happens according to the deeds of the wicked, and there are wicked men to whom it happens according to the deeds of the righteous" (8:14). Without divine intervention in the affairs of men there cannot be any notion of divine retribution, nor, for that matter, any active principle of redemptive activity by God. Ultimately, the writer of Ecclesiastes rejects all doctrine and identifies life's goal as simply survival with a measure of contentment.

The specific passage under consideration here, 3:16–22, I take to be representative of the book. The writer begins with the observation that even in the place of justice and righteousness there is wickedness. This is not a cynical statement but apparently a simple observation of fact. The Revised Standard Version translates v. 17 as if the writer believed in his heart that God will judge the righteous and the wicked. Scott understands this to be the writer speaking to himself, inwardly recalling what is normally taught in Israel. He translates vs. 17–18 as follows: "I quoted to myself, 'God will judge between the just man and the evildoer,' since there is a destined time for every experience and an appointed moment for every deed. Then I said to myself, 'It is on men's own account, that God may show [them] that they are only animals.' "[20] Scott interprets the two verses as first raising and then rejecting the orthodox retributional position. The ultimate conclusion of the writer of the passage is really that contained in vs. 18 ff.—since death and dust are inevitable, man truly is no better off than the beasts. Therefore, "there is nothing better than that a man should enjoy his work, for that is his lot" (3:22). The logical thrust of the passage leads thus toward the position that life is to be lived within its limitations of understanding and expectation. Ideology is to be rejected, as is any idealism which makes assumptions about interventions in human affairs by a perfectly just and merciful God. Joy is possible only if one does not seek perfected wisdom or justice. As for death, it is a demonstration neither of justice nor of injustice, because all life is bound for extinction anyway.

The rejection of the retributional ideology and the doubt that any successful style of life can be built upon convictions about God's absolute attributes is the line of thought developed most fully in the Book of Job. To that book I shall now turn, seeking to present its complex argument in a highly compressed and schematic way.

The first question that springs to mind as one sees the righteous man Job sitting in agony and despair on the dunghill is the basic one. Is there then a God at all? To this Job and all the other characters of the book give a firmly affirmative answer. The ancient folktale which forms the outer framework of the book (chs. 1 to 2; 42:7–17) and the massive intervening dialogues and theophany are in agreement on this point as well. There is a God who created the world and is capable of changing the course of events in it as he wills. Why then has Job's tragic situation come about? In answer to this, the book affirms that within this world absurd and inexplicable evil and suffering exist. The folktale cares for the external

and public dimension of this truth. The dialogues and Yahweh's speeches (chs. 38 to 41) look to the private, intellectual,
and psychological dimension. Both dimensions, however,
make clear that such inexplicable evil raises a profound problem for the reward-and-punishment schemes of the Deuteronomic writings and the Psalms of the Two Ways.

Perhaps God is evil and cruel and simply arbitrarily gives
rise to evil and injustice? Although Job's friends resolutely
reject such an idea (34:10–15), Job himself seems to reckon
with the possibility. In the famous passage which some have
understood to be the moment of Job's sin, Job cries out: "I am
blameless; I regard not myself; I loathe my life. It is all one;
therefore I say, he destroys both the blameless and the
wicked. When disaster brings sudden death, he mocks at the
calamity of the innocent." (9:21–23.) Yet in the balance, the
idea that God is evil certainly is rejected by all speakers.

Perhaps, then, God just doesn't care? Perhaps he is deaf
and dumb or else unconcerned? That God is silent throughout the drama is certainly remarkable. Even Elihu notes it
(34:29). But that silence is swept away in the great theophany
of chs. 38 to 41. The theophany also sweeps away the possibility that God is unconcerned and that a mediator (9:33–35)
would be necessary to cause God to take Job's plight seriously. God does take Job's plight so seriously that, in the last
analysis, he manifests himself to Job personally and instructs
him at length.

But still Job suffers and the reason is not found. Can it be
that such an evil situation is, after all, a punishment? Job's
suffering certainly has the outer and public appearance of
punishment. The details of his loss of property and family and
his physical illness very much parallel description of the accursed person given in Deut. 28:15–68. Zophar notes this
(11:1–6). Job himself makes it explicit in his bitter cry, "God
has cast me into the mire, and I have become like dust and
ashes" (30:19). And yet in Job's case no transgression warrant-
ing such extreme punishment was committed, as Job swears

in 31:16–23. Since it is a universally accepted premise of the law that the punishment should fit the crime, either Job has committed some horrendous secret crime—which the readers know he has not—or else something has gone awry with God's retributional policy.

Is it conceivable that God is simply powerless to prevent Job's kind of situation from arising? We know from the narrative setting of the book that God is not to be seen as the author of Job's sufferings even though he permits them to take place. However, because the narrative stage setting of the folktale ought not to be taken as the most basic component of the meaning of the book as we now have it, we also cannot say that Satan is the author of suffering. Even if the source of the suffering is unknown, should not God redress the wrong done to an innocent victim, especially given his acknowledged justice and omnipotence? Job presses his legal claim (13:13–23) along these lines. If Psalm 1 and even the Deuteronomic covenant formulation were adequate expressions of God's legal commitment, he would be acting in an illicit fashion to permit these events to happen to Job.

But he does permit them, a brute fact which at least suggests that legal language is inadequate to describe God's way of dealing with evil. God's hands are not tied by a curse-and-blessing, reward-and-punishment scheme which would require him to reward a good person or punish an evil one in necessary response to that person's works. Nor can an argument from God's transcendent attribute of omnipotence provide any basis for solving this problem. In this the Book of Job appears to agree completely with the position of Ecclesiastes.

The penultimate dilemma, then, is this: Job's suffering continues and God, who is neither evil, unconcerned, nor incapable of preventing it, nonetheless permits it to do so.

The dialogues of the Book of Job explore some other possibilities for understanding suffering which are perhaps tangential to our main concern: (1) The possibility that suffering

is truly meaningless is not hinted at here as it is in Ecclesiastes. Neither is it possible to say in any satisfying way
why it is meaningful. (2) The contention that suffering is
God's chastening unto perfection, which is the general view
of Eliphaz (5:17–24) and of Elihu (33:19–33) is finally rejected. (3) The stoic resignation of the patient Job of the
folktale who, in the face of God's incomprehensibility, says,
"The LORD gave and the LORD has taken away; blessed be
the name of the LORD" (1:21), is finally rejected in favor of
hard intellectual activity aimed at making sense of the experience of sufferings. (4) Finally, the possibility of an eternal
reward for righteous sufferers in a life beyond this vale of
tears is not even seriously raised. The much-disputed text of
19:25–27 is now almost universally understood not to refer to
the possibility of resurrection and spiritual reunion with God.

The ultimate dilemma of the book is created when Job
repents (42:5–6). At this moment his suffering ends and a
liberal indemnity is given by God, who shows that he can
give as well as take away. But this restoration is not a reward,
since Job was not vindicated. His repentance seems to be the
most proximate cause of the happy conclusion in its final
form. Yet the question remains, What was the nature of this
repentance? Was it an internalization of the reality of God's
power? "I know that thou canst do all things and that no
purpose of thine can be thwarted" (42:2). Or was it above all
an acknowledgment of the dependability of God's presence?
"I had heard of thee by the hearing of the ear, but now my
eye sees thee" (42:5). Whatever the writer's precise intention
in tying the repentance to the restoration, the process of the
book as a whole would appear to be the radicalization of Job's
view of God as retributor and redeemer. By outer pressure
of events and inner hard intellectual and spiritual activity,
Job is forced to recognize his subjectness and his mortality,
to admit the ultimate inaccessibility and even unaccountabil-
ity of the transcendent deity. His major discovery is that God
wills to be for his people, and that as people discover him to

be an immanent deity and confess his power to support them they can in fact overcome the tragedies of the world. With this radicalization Job does overcome, a victory which the final writer allows the folk-ending to dramatize, but which is already vivid in the repentance of 42:1–6.

Here, then, is my understanding of the response of the Book of Job to the problem presented by the righteous sufferer. In contrast to the retributional perspective which would tend to interpret the suffering as punishment for unfaith or sin, Job affirms the impossibility of basing a theology of reward-and-punishment, retribution and restoration, upon an appeal to God's transcendent attributes of power and justice. One must acknowledge that God remains unchanged and forever true to himself. But God also turned his children loose in a world which is radically other from him, radically separated from his transcendent attributes. In that world a struggle for redemption is taking place. God is engaged in that same struggle alongside us. He will emerge victorious—though that statement points to the eschatological dimension of the struggle which is not developed in the Book of Job. The world in which the struggle and the victory take place is his world, upheld in truth by his transcendent power exercised in his providential care. But in Job the stress is on his action alongside us in the struggle. Only such an interpretation will adequately account for Job's suffering. The evil which we encounter in the figure of Job, and indeed in our own experience, may be in fact absurd and meaningless. But because God is with us, because he is Immanuel, it can become meaningful as it is overcome. In that, and not in the retributional scheme, is there hope and consolation in the face of suffering. Finally, the assurance that God is Immanuel opens out once again to the redemption motif in the Scriptures.

Direction

Ecclesiastes and Job strike major blows against the Old Testament ideology of divine retribution and leave in something of a shambles the motif so extensively employed in the Deuteronomists' work and so neatly epitomized in Psalm 1. And yet the position in which we are left by this turn of events in the ongoing dialectic between the retributional motif and its opposites is not entirely happy. Ecclesiastes alone would leave us with neither confidence in the vindication of God's justice nor hope in the ultimate triumph of his mercy. Job leaves us with a strong assurance that God, the immanent one, is for us in our suffering and despair. The book opens out to the redemption motif in the Scriptures, but at what point can that strand be picked up again?

My own answer to this begins with a sentence also to be found in the Book of Job: "Behold, the fear of the Lord, that is wisdom; and to depart from evil is understanding" (28:28). When that is repeated after an experience such as Job's has run its full course, it begins to suggest some positive next steps. It begins to suggest an affirmation of life, even with its anguishes, and a glad response to the God who shows himself to be the lover and supporter and healer of one's own life. It suggests a life-style based not upon fear of God's perfect justice and his determination to exact "an eye for an eye," but rather upon awe and wonder at God's willingness to be *for* us, even on a dunghill. Such a life-style responds to God not with scrupulosity but with an ebullience of giving and loving and acting on his behalf. Not to move out in this way from the experience of being human is to experience something else: a hellish and boundless loss, the loss of the opportunity to respond, the loss of the chance to have life and to have it more abundantly.

Obviously, this witness of the books of Ecclesiastes and Job moves back into the main sweep of the redemption motif of the Bible. It blends well into its comprehensive dramatic structure and compares authentically with the Word of God at the center. For it is as unthinkable to those who know the crucified and risen Christ as it is to the repentant and truly wise Job that meaningless torture of any individual could be attributed to God, or that God could be unaware and absent when it takes place.

CHRISTOLOGY AND THE THEME OF RETRIBUTION

Text

16 For God so loved the world that he gave his only Son, that whoever believes in him should not perish but have eternal life. 17 For God sent the Son into the world, not to condemn the world, but that the world might be saved through him. 18 He who believes in him is not condemned; he who does not believe is condemned already, because he has not believed in the name of the only Son of God. 19 And this is the judgment, that the light has come into the world, and men loved darkness rather than light, because their deeds were evil. 20 For every one who does evil hates the light, and does not come to the light, lest his deeds should be exposed. 21 But he who does what is true comes to the light, that it may be clearly seen that his deeds have been wrought in God.

—John 3:16–21

Discussion

The Gospel of John is generally thought to have been written at the turn of the second century A.D., possibly as a Christian response to the challenge of gnosticism.[21] The Gospel may be seen as addressing the problem of gnosticism in two ways. First, it adopts a great deal of the imagery of gnosticism, including the antithetical dualities of light and darkness, heaven and world, good and evil. At the same time, it rejects the fundamental presupposition of gnosticism, namely, that reality is divided into two warring principali-

ties. The ongoing struggle of faith in gnosticism is to release
the divine element trapped in the evil material cosmos so
that it may return to its own sphere. Although John regards
the world as fallen, the redemption of its people is accomplished not by their efforts to be released from it but by their
decision to embrace what God has already done on their
behalf.

What God has done for the world has been done through
his Word, incarnate in Jesus of Nazareth. The purpose of the
Fourth Gospel is not primarily to report what Jesus said and
did about a number of matters, as is the purpose of the Synop-
tic Gospels. Rather, its every effort is to let the reader know
who this man is. No longer are the miracle stories, for example, signs of the power of God over Satan. No longer are
Jesus' teachings in the first instance instructions in a new
Way. Miracles and sayings are recounted for the purpose of
identifying this man as the Son of God. The task of John's
Gospel is the development of thoroughgoing Christology.

The passage of John's Gospel that I have chosen to examine, central as it is to understanding Johannine Christology,
bears on the question of retribution in tension with the motif
of redemption. It begins with the famous encapsulated gospel of v. 16. The "world" into which God gave his only-
begotten son is that entity which stands over against heaven
in the Fourth Gospel. The coming of the Son into this world
provided an opportunity for people to believe or not to believe, and so to perish or not to perish. The event of the
incarnation occurred at a specific point in time (*edōken*, "[he]
gave," is in the aorist indicative), but the significance which
flows from every decision made in the face of that event is
open-ended toward the future (*mē apolētai*, "[he] should not
perish," is in the subjunctive mood). All those in the world
"who believe in him" (the formulation is participial and the
action is continuous in the present) "[may] have eternal life"
(again the verb is subjunctive, and also in the present tense).

Clearly the strand of present and open-ended action which

began even before our pericope opens (see v. 15) continues and runs through the entire passage. Belief and unbelief, salvation and condemnation, are all taking place right now in the presence of the mission and work of Christ. In short, as Bultmann has long ago pointed out, an eschatological crisis is a present, not a future, reality for those who confront Jesus Christ.

In v. 17, God "sent" his son as a past event in time, but the judging of the world and the saving of the world are expressed in the subjunctive mood. Thus, again, the events which flow from God's act open out into uncharted and unlimited future possibilities.

The Evangelist then proceeds to show (v. 18) that the very act which makes possible the salvation of the world is also the occasion of its judgment. If a person who encounters the Christ in the present moment believes in him and accepts his lordship, that person's future is already established and settled. Conversely, a decision against the Christ here and now also settles the future. The decisive eschatological judgment is now. The sequence of verbal tenses in this verse, from the present "is not condemned" to the perfect passive "has been condemned already," seems to suggest that the noncondemnation of the believer is an ongoing continuous reality, whereas the condemnation of the unbeliever is a completed act. (The *New English Bible* puts it cogently by translating, "The man who puts his faith in him does not come under judgement; but the unbeliever has already been judged. . . .") This is why it is so important to recognize in the Christ a constant, present eschatological event. As long as that event is in the midst of the world, the possibility of moving from unbelief to belief always exists.

The passage shows two ways in which the Fourth Gospel radicalizes traditional eschatology. First, the moment of decision and of judgment is not at the last day but now—whenever a human being faces the person and claim of Christ. Second, the opportunity to make a positive decision is never

removed. Far from being a once-for-all distant cosmic encounter, the moment of truth between a person and the Son
of God can and does happen daily, in the present mundane
existence.

In v. 19 the imagery of light and darkness is introduced,
but the stress on the judgment or *krisis* brought on by the
present moment of decision remains. The individual is confronted by the choice of whether to draw near and be exposed to the light or to remain in the former darkness. What
one does in relation to the light reveals who one really is, and
sets the direction for the future. Unless a person makes a
basic decision to withdraw from the light, that person may
perhaps draw near and move away many times in the oscilla-
tion of belief and unbelief. However, the light, the eschatological *krisis,* remains as an abiding opportunity for salvation.

Bultmann finds no judging, retributive role for the Son in
the Christology of this passage, or in the rest of John for that
matter.[22] Jesus' mission, an event in history, because it forces
a decision with implications for the near and distant future,
is also an eschatological event. The event itself is an event of
love. The fact that that love also becomes a judgment on
those who refuse it is their own responsibility, not Christ's.
Because the Son has no future role as Judge at a great Retribution, inasmuch as the eschatology of John knows of no
substantial futuristic dimension, he is never really pictured as
one who judges and condemns people.

The question now arises, how does this Christology of John
3:16 ff., taken as illustrative of the entire Gospel, compare
with other Christologies within the Gospels themselves, particularly at the point of the judging and redeeming work of
Christ? Obviously, the view on the matter contained in John
is utterly different from that contained, for example, in the
little apocalypses of Matt., chs. 24 to 25; Mark, ch. 13; Luke
21:5–36. In the latter, as an aspect of what is sometimes
called the Jewish-Christian apocalypse,[23] Jesus is identified
with the coming Son of Man whose appearance is to signal

a general resurrection, a world judgment, and an eternal rejection of those who are condemned on account of their unbelief and unfaithfulness.

But what was Jesus' own view of his role as judge and mediator of divine retribution? W. Kümmel argues that Jesus' own view of his role as judge (or better, *krisis* bringer) was closer to the outlook of the Fourth Gospel than to that of the apocalyptic texts in the Synoptics. Cautious as he is in claiming to discover elements of Jesus' own self-understanding on the matter, Kümmel does point out that Jesus taught that persons are distinguished now by their acceptance or rejection of himself. Acceptance of the man Jesus now means "adherence to the coming Kingdom of God at work in advance already in the present."[24] In contrast to the picture given in the Fourth Gospel, the Jesus of the Synoptics expects an eschatological day of judgment at which human actions will be examined, and asserts that every person's response to Jesus' own person and ministry will be of central significance for them on that Day of Reckoning.[25] Jesus evidently believed that the truth of these convictions would be demonstrated by divine action within the lifetimes of his hearers. In that, he was wrong.[26] But he rightly saw an eschaton as a future event, bound together with and confirmed by the events of his own ministry. Kümmel, in opposition to many scholars, argues that Jesus did not teach that the Kingdom of Heaven is an invisible but ongoing reality from his own time until its full manifestation in the Eschaton, and something in which believers may participate now. The Kingdom of Heaven is visible in proleptic form only in the person and work of Jesus. Between his time and the Last Day, the believer's task, if Kümmel's understanding of Jesus' own "Christology" is correct, is to make the ultimately significant positive response to Jesus and then to live faithfully and expectantly in between the times, following his teachings. At the Parousia all who decide for him will be vindicated by Jesus when he returns as the eschatological judge.[27]

Another approach to the question of the judging function in New Testament Christologies, especially in Jesus' own, is that of E. Käsemann.[28] If asked to describe Jesus' self-understanding about his eschatological role as mediator of divine retribution, Käsemann would begin his answer by saying, "His own preaching was not constitutively stamped by apocalyptic but proclaimed the immediate nearness of God."[29] Only subsequently did two parties appear whose controversy over the proper stance of the believer in between the times can be recovered from the gospel tradition. The early Christian enthusiasts, whose proclivity to exercise now the powers of the Messianic Kingdom is revealed in a passage such as Matt. 7:22–23,[30] argued with the rigoristic Jewish-Christians and their eschatological *jus talionis* (Matt. 7:2; 23:12). The central message of the teaching of the latter was that the future epiphany of Jesus as the Son of Man would proclaim to all the world the righteousness of God through the destruction of the wicked and unbelievers and the salvation of righteous believers. The salvation and destruction, though taking place in the distant future, are apprehended already in the decision which one makes in the face of the present promise and threat posed by Jesus himself, as Matt. 10:32 shows.[31]

In a second study, Käsemann sees a development in Jesus' own thinking about the apocalyptic dimension of his ministry. Jesus began with the same glowing near expectation of the Kingdom as did John the Baptist,[32] but the evidence suggests that he later broke with that view and began to press instead the inescapable nearness and distance of the Kingdom of God. The nearness cuts against the asceticism represented by the Baptist, diverting the focus to an emphasis on love as the appropriate Christian response. The inescapable distance of the Kingdom gives rise to an eschatological reservation which cautions that the Kingdom is not yet here in all of its fullness. This dimension of Jesus' teaching is summed up by Käsemann: "The repentance which [Jesus], too, demands

takes its bearing not on wrath but on grace, so that he summons man to the daily service of God as if no shadow lay upon
the world and God were not unapproachable."[33] In fact, God
is unapproachable, in the sense that the full relationship between God and man has not yet been consummated. But a
life of obedience is still possible in the present.

In his first article, Käsemann reached essentially the same
point as did Kümmel and in a sense even Bultmann, in
attributing to the very earliest gospel tradition, perhaps even
to Jesus himself, the conviction that the event of Jesus' own
life and ministry is the original eschatological *krisis* in the
face of which every person has to make a decision. The problem of Jesus' judging role now and in the future is compli-
cated by the rise of post-Easter Christian apocalypticism.
This movement was undergirded by the church's identification of Jesus with the futuristic Jewish figure of the Son of
Man. This identification, though indicative of the totality in
which Jesus, to those who knew him as the risen Lord,
fulfilled and comprehended Old Testament messianic expectation, also created a severe problem; for Jesus did not do all
that the Son of Man of Jewish expectation was supposed to
do. According to Dan. 7:13–14, he was supposed to come
"with the clouds of heaven" to receive "dominion and glory
and kingdom." According to such texts as Enoch 62:5; 69:
27 ff.; 50:1–3; IV Ezra 13:35–38, he was supposed to judge the
world at the end of history and to inaugurate a new age. If
Jesus is also the Son of Man, must he too not do all this at some
future Parousia? The answer of the Christian apocalyptists of
the early church was, of course, yes. After this link was made,
the church had to develop language to cope with its implications. That language is incorporated into the Gospels in the
little apocalypses and elsewhere. Jesus' own teaching regarding his judging role should be kept strictly separated from
this material.

But is there no continuity, then, between Jesus' own Christology, so to speak, and that of the eschatological interpreters

of his work? To that question, too, the answer is, "Yes, there is." In the words and work of Jesus there is evidence of a gracious breaking into the world by God, a movement against all in law and religion and culture that makes God foreign and distant and hostile. At the same time, there is implicit in Jesus' own preaching a future hope with which the subsequent apocalyptic development is in a legitimate continuity. It is the hope that every individual can look toward a kingdom of freedom which is like Jesus' own freedom from sin and death. Yet, in Jesus' own message there is little or nothing about eschatological judgment. If Käsemann is right, Jesus' is a modest Christology because it does not make the identification of himself with the apocalyptic Son of Man. It is a Christology which says the Kingdom of Heaven (though not necessarily the Parousia) is near us, but at the same moment God is not yet approachable in the ultimate sense. Jesus is thus a teacher of evangelical tidings. Because the Kingdom of Heaven is near, it is possible to enter into its life and participate in it now, embracing its joy and displaying its redemptive qualities even as Jesus himself does. Although the early Christians, moving back to the vision of the Baptist and the terms of the prevailing Jewish expectation, tied all these teachings of the "at-handness" of the Kingdom to an imminent judgment day, Jesus did not share their view of the ultimate significance of his ministry: "He overturns the Baptist's message at a decisive point, inasmuch as the repentance which he, too, demands takes its bearings not on wrath but on grace."[34]

Direction

Beginning with a text from the Fourth Gospel, I have reviewed several Christologies present in the gospel tradition, including scholarly reconstructions of Jesus' own, with an eye toward their respective contributions to the ongoing Biblical dialectic between the motifs of divine retribution and redemption. Now I must touch again upon the question of priority. Here, at the veritable center of the Scriptures against which all other canonical motifs and teachings must be checked, appear a multiplicity of ways of understanding the role which the Christ must play in rewarding and punishing. Which mode of understanding will it be? Will it be Jesus' own Christology or some other?

First, we cannot successfully use Jesus' own Christology alone as a starting point, for the simple reason that we cannot be sure we have accurately recovered it. The picture of Jesus given in the gospel consists of a series of icons, holy word pictures, carefully crafted and framed, which the early church has given us. The church gave us exactly what it wanted us to hear from and about Jesus; however, from such material Jesus' own thinking about a theological motif as complex as the principle of divine retribution can hardly be reconstructed. Second, neither are we absolutely bound by any other Christology of the New Testament as we set about building a Biblical-theological treatment of the two entangled motifs of divine retribution and the divine intention to redeem the world. Paul's Christology in I Cor., ch. 15, does not bind us absolutely; neither does John's in 3:16–21, nor the "Jewish-Christian" apocalyptic Christology identified by Kümmel, Käsemann, and many others. Third, we neither can nor should combine them all into a unified synthetic Christology. At the point of doing systematic theology we may have to come down to the point of developing a single, if highly articulated, Christological position. However, at the point of doing the task of Biblical theology we cannot allege a unity of Biblical viewpoint where none exists. This is not to say that there is always a total cleavage between one Biblical treatment of an issue such as Christology and another. Certain underlying convictions will inform all interpretations. The New Testament will not say "He is Judge" in one place and "He is Redeemer" in another, and do so from totally separated fundamental assumptions. Informing both will be the common commitment, "Jesus Christ is the risen Lord."

One might say that Christ himself transcends any one strand of interpretation of his nature and work. The church recognizes this when it points to a kerygmatic formulation from which no variation can be admitted, "Jesus Christ is the risen Lord." However, that irreducible formula is not in itself as amplified as any adequate Christology has to be in order to meet the ongoing needs of the church. Hence the rise of various amplifications, and also the problem which we confront. What are we then to do?

In developing my fourth methodological principle in Chapter III, I argued that interpretation within the context of the canon means building outward toward contemporary needs from one of the possible Biblical starting points which we choose. At the same time we must allow all the other points of view to check and correct the interpretation.[35] This is quite a different approach from one which would claim that all the New Testament Christologies, for example, are ultimately presenting the same basic message. The choice of the starting point emerges out of a dialectic within the interpreter's own mind, between the evident theological priorities within Scripture itself and the situation of the people of God, including the interpreter, in and for whom the interpretation is being developed.

Though I struggle to check every interpretative judgment against the actual text, the overall architecture, and the all-important Christological center of Scripture, it can scarcely be otherwise that my choice of a starting point will be affected by where I am as a believer in a twentieth-century American historical and theological context. Here I am, brought up in the main-line, Protestant tradition, struggling to find a *legitimate Biblical* way of encompassing and limiting the well-known Biblical affirmation of the reality of divine wrath and retribution. Why should I do that? Why can't I be comfortable with simply noting that these themes of divine wrath-retribution and mercy-redemption appear to be balanced and of more-or-less equal importance in Scripture? Why can't I be content with the teachings of the Augsburg and Westminster Confessions that the destiny of some is eternal life and of others everlasting punishment? Part of the answer lies in my own existential experience with my White Anglo-Saxon Protestant co-religionists. For generations we have suffered under the weight of too much ideology of retribution, too much guilt and too much punishment, and too little recognition of the freedom of the gospel in the hope of redemption. I cite this only as an example of the personal and human component in an interpreter's choice among objectively identifiable Biblical options from which to begin to build toward a relevant and constructive and contemporary theology. Not only individuals but whole generations work this way. Liberal theology died under the impact of the Hitler era when interpreters began to work from a different set of Biblical assertions about God's justice and wrath than had been used earlier. Yet, thankfully, the individual judgments of interpreters continued to add crucial insights to the general trend. For example, Karl Barth, who was preeminent in the '30s and '40s in holding up anew the Biblical themes of responsibility and obedience, also insisted on affirming God's power ultimately to comprehend his retributive judgment within the larger framework of his purpose to redeem his entire creation.[36]

God May Be Everything to Every One

Text

20 But in fact Christ has been raised from the dead, the first fruits of those who have fallen asleep. 21 For as by a man came death, by a man has come also the resurrection of the dead. 22 For as in Adam all die, so also in Christ shall all be made alive. 23 But each in his own order: Christ the first fruits, then at his coming those who belong to Christ. 24 Then comes the end, when he delivers the kingdom to God the Father after

destroying every rule and every authority and power. 25 For he must reign until he has put all his enemies under his feet. 26 The last enemy to be destroyed is death. 27 "For God has put all things in subjection under his feet." But when it says, "All things are put in subjection under him," it is plain that he is excepted who put all things under him. 28 When all things are subjected to him, then the Son himself will also be subjected to him who put all things under him, that God may be everything to every one.

—I Corinthians 15:20–28

Discussion

The setting and background of Paul's first epistle to the Corinthian church are well known. Commonly dated in late A.D. 53 or early 54,[37] the epistle is universally recognized as from the apostle himself. Foremost among the many concerns which the epistle addresses is the problem of factionalism at the Corinthian church. Paul writes against one faction as opponents, a group who are commonly identified as "enthusiasts." These Christians felt that the new aeon had already arrived and that they, as the body of Christ, were already a transfigured angelic body of some kind. Perhaps it was they who denied the resurrection from the dead (15:12), on the ground that believers already enjoyed a fully transformed eschatological existence. Whether these were Gentiles in the Corinthian church who had received the faith in a pentecostal outpouring of the Spirit, or apocalyptically oriented Jewish Christians, or proto-gnostics, no one knows for certain. Against their enthusiasm, however, Paul was moved to state his "eschatological reservation": Yes, we expect a full manifestation of the liberty of the sons of God, but no, we are not there yet. Part of the passage under consideration here (vs. 23–28, which together with 15:50–57 has been postulated to be Paul's edited version of an existing apocalypse[38]) talks about the Eschaton as a future event. In that

sense it both corrects those who would say that the End has
already happened in the resurrection of Christ and the bap-
tism of the church by his Spirit, and also provides for all
believers a very broad vision of what the fulfillment of God's
purpose means.

In v. 20, Paul announced a finished and perfected reality
whose results now are in effect: "Christ has been raised from
the dead." "Those who have fallen asleep," a familiar Pauline
synonym for the dead, now have a resurrected representative as their "first fruits." Verses 21–22 form a couplet in
which the significance of Christ's first passion and resurrection for all mankind is twice identified.How seriously should
we take "all," repeated twice in v. 22? Clearly, "all" who die
in Adam includes the entire human race from the beginning
to the end of time (see 5:12). But does "all" mean something
different in the second part of the verse? Common sense
would suggest that two words used in such synonymous parallelism would mean the same thing. Some interpreters escape the dangers in such an understanding by using the two
prepositional phrases *(en tō Adam . . . en tō Christō)* as modi-
fiers of the two occurrences of "all." The contrast would then
be between "all (who are) in Adam" and "all (who are) in
Christ." With the additional assumption that "all who are in
Adam" by definition includes the entire fallen human race,
but that "all who are in Christ" includes only those who have
believed in him, these commentators conclude that the two
stichs of v. 22 refer to different groups of persons.[39] It seems
highly unlikely to me, however, that Paul would have con-
structed the verse in this way had he meant to refer to two
groups of different scope and character. As it stands, the
word order suggests that the prepositional phrases "in
Adam" and "in Christ" should be understood as indicating
instrumentality or agency. "In Adam" means "through the
agency of Adam" or "by Adam"; "in Christ" suggests
"through the Christic action" or "by Christ."[40] This is supported by the clear double reference to the agency of "man"

in v. 21 (although the preposition *dia* is used here). If v. 22 is essentially a restatement of v. 21, the stress would seem to fall upon the respective agency of Adam and Christ, and "all" would seem to refer to the humankind for whom their agency is exercised.

One might argue that these two verses are merely affirming a stage in the sequence of eschatological events which appears quite commonly in the Jewish and Christian apocalyptic literature, namely, the general resurrection of all the dead just prior to the Judgment. This argument, too, encounters difficulty with the simple parallelism in each of the two verses. The death that comes to all in Adam is pervasive, even ontological; are we not to understand the resurrection that comes through Christ to have the same fundamental character? Does Paul not mean that what Christ does for mankind as a whole cancels and perfectly overcomes what Adam did? If the death which comes through Adam is the inexorable result of sin, is Paul not teaching that the life which comes through Christ is the equally inexorable and inescapable result of the overcoming of sin in the judgment which he underwent in his own body on behalf of all mankind?

Verses 23 ff. introduce the Pauline apocalyptic interpretation. There is an order of events of which Christ's resurrection is the first (v. 23a). Against the enthusiasts, Paul contends that other events are yet to come. This includes the second resurrection, of "those who belong to Christ," at the moment of his Parousia. This second stage is also recognized in the apocalyptic scheme of the book of Revelation, at 20:4. There, however, a thousand-year reign of Christ and the saints intervenes; in this text, Paul seems to know of no such millennium. Instead, the third eschatological event follows immediately (v. 24). "Then comes the end *(to telos)*" is a much-debated phrase. Barrett rejects the argument that this might mean "the rest of humanity" (Lietzmann), saying that no notion of the salvation of nonbelievers is contained in this verse. For him, this stage in Paul's apocalyptic order merely refers to the resurrection of those who were dead in Christ (v. 23c having referred to those Christians who were alive at the time of the Parousia—a sequence which would appear to be the reverse of that proposed in the apocalyptic sequence underlying I Thess. 4:16).[41] Others, however, understand the third step to include the resurrection of all humanity (the second resurrection of Rev. 20:7–15), to the end that all might be saved. Arndt and Gingrich, discussing the meaning of *to tagma,* the "order" of v. 23a, remark: "According to I Cor. 15:23 f. the gift of life is given to various ones in turn . . . , and at various times. One view is that in this connection Paul distinguishes three groups: Christ, who already possesses life, the Christians, who will receive it at his second coming, and the rest of humanity *(telos),* who will receive it when death, as the last of God's enemies, is destroyed."[42]

The passage concludes, vs. 24b–28, with a discussion of the conquest by Christ of all the powers of the cosmos which enslave and deflect the world's goodness, and the subjugation of all things, even death, to Christ. Finally, in the strange subordinationist Christology of v. 28, the Son himself "is subjected" (passive) to God, "that God may be everything to every one" (v. 28). A clearer statement of a vision of the universal salvation of the entire created universe in all of its material, human, and spiritual dimensions, can hardly be imagined!

Direction

I shall conclude this discussion of the famous Pauline affirmation of the ultimate triumph of the divine redemption scheme by advancing and briefly defending four theses concerning the universalistic dimension in Paul's view of salvation. First, *Paul cannot be called a straightforward and consistent universalist in his eschatological expectation.* This text is, after all, only one small segment of a large corpus of writings attributed to Paul. Here and elsewhere he considered judgment and the destruction of evil to be a given and essential part of both the present and future activity of God. In I Cor. 3:17 he speaks of the retributive judgment which comes to those who misuse the body; in 6:9–11 he announces that the unrighteous and immoral will not inherit the Kingdom of God. Though he does not here threaten them with burning in the lake of fire in the manner of the author of the Christian apocalypse (Rev. 21:8), they are judged nonetheless. Even those who profane the Eucharist may die (11:27–30), though the punishment seems to be regarded more as a natural consequence of the sin than as a direct retributive act of God. Paul's strongest expression of the motif of divine vengeance through the judging work of the Lord Jesus at his second coming is found in II Thess. 1:6–9.[43]

Second, *The epistles nonetheless contain inescapable evidences that Paul could conceive of the ultimate redemption of the entire universe, and that because of the utterly new situation created by the New Adam.* We might label this view the "adamic Christology" of Paul, because Christ is presented as the antithesis to the old Adam in both of the key texts in which this idea is explored, Rom. 5:18–21 (see 11:32), and the passage here considered, I Cor. 15:20–28. (The theme is also echoed in the deutero-Pauline texts Eph. 1:9–10 and Col. 1:19–20.) When he uses this imagery, Paul obviously wants to underscore the vast historical scope of the great drama of redemption, that framework in which the Bible presents mankind's long struggle to undo the curse of Babel and to find the way back to Eden. Christ opens the way into the new paradise beyond the Eschaton, just as Adam was sent on his way from Eden after the Fall.

But how can Paul assert two such fundamentally irreconcilable doctrines, even granting that he might have placed the emphasis differently to different audiences confronting different challenges to the faith? One answer to this question would involve a hypothesis which can be given only minimal textual support. Paul could have amalgamated the two different motifs—divine retribution against sinners both now and at the Eschaton; and the universal redemption of the cosmos —by anticipating a three-stage apocalyptic sequence in which an initial Parousia and judgment are followed by an indeterminately long interval and then, in turn, by a general resurrection and redemption of all persons. Such a sequence would imply an intermediate state for the dead, during which the unrighteous could be purged in preparation for their ultimate salvation.[44] Such a sequence might barely be hinted at in I Cor. 15:20–28, if the period between the Parousia of v. 23 and the final subjugation of all things, including death, to the Christ (v. 26) is understood as the period of purging for those who did not rise with Christ at the first resurrection. However, too many pieces are missing here and throughout the Pauline corpus to affirm that Paul foresaw this particular series of apocalyptic events or reconciled his two conflicting convictions in this way.

Thus, in assembling the Biblical data bearing on the motif of divine retribution, *we are forced simply to leave Paul's two dimensions of thought on the matter side by side in the tension in which they now stand.* Other considerations, including the influence of the Christological center of the Scripture, will determine which Pauline theme will ultimately be given the greater priority in a comprehensive treatment on the motif. My own view, not yet fully articulated, is that the vision of universal redemption glimpsed in I Cor., ch. 15, better accords with the kerygma of that center than does the vision of ultimate destruction of parts of the cosmos at the hands of a Christ who is unable fully to complete his mission of salvation. Because of my experience as a modern Christian who has lived in the Auschwitz era and who therefore considers the salient Biblical theme of divine justice to be crucial, I will also affirm the possibility that persons can truly and painfully reject God's intention to redeem them.[45] But can persons reject God's love eternally, thus defeating his purpose by becoming permanently alienated and separated from him? Paul seems to discount that possibility in I Cor. 15:20–28, and we must take him seriously in this. Perhaps we can only leave ourselves firmly impaled on this dilemma, taking as our watchword for this final stage of our way a phrase from the Proposed Confession of the Presbyterian Church in the United States: "We affirm that evil is God's enemy as well as ours. In Christ God shared our agony over it. He works continually to overcome it. The last word will be God's 'Good!' "[46]

THE GATES THAT NEVER SHUT

Text

31 Another parable he put before them, saying, "The kingdom of heaven is like a grain of mustard seed which a man took and sowed in his field; 32 it is the smallest of all seeds, but when it has grown it is the greatest of shrubs and becomes a tree, so that the birds of the air come and make nests in its branches. . . ." 44 "The kingdom of heaven is like treasure hidden in a field, which a man found and covered up; then in his joy he goes and sells all that he has and buys that field. 45 Again, the kingdom of heaven is like a merchant in search of fine pearls, 46 who, on finding one pearl of great value, went and sold all that he had and bought it."

—*Matthew 13:31–32, 44–46*

Discussion

In this final examination of texts I want to look at these parables. They are illustrative of one aspect of Jesus' teaching about the nature of the Kingdom of Heaven. We will examine some of the other New Testament eschatological materials as well. The goal will be to try to determine whether their primary purpose is to announce judgment or redemption, or whether they have some other task.

The first of the parables of the Kingdom cited here (Matt.

13:31–32) conveys the single point that what is now found as
a tiny beginning will, in the eschatological age, become a
huge reality. The mustard seed is going to become the largest
of shrubs, a veritable tree. Nevertheless, everything that the
full-grown tree becomes turns out to have been already incipient in the tiny seed. The hearer is not challenged by the
parable to nurture and care for some inward personal confession of faith until it flowers into eschatological fulfillment.
Instead of stressing the process of growth, the parable con-
centrates solely on the end result.[47] Inasmuch as the end of
the matter is already implicit in the beginning, those who
live in between the time of the planting and the full manifestation can, if they have eyes to see, already perceive at least
the outlines of the end. So the end inevitably does affect the
style of those who live along the way, even though their
living cannot affect the end. Furthermore, the outcome of
the growth is inevitable—the bush will out! That too must
affect how people live in between the times, insofar as they
realize what is going on and choose to live in harmony with
it. The implications for living in between the times are not
spelled out further here, but from the post-Easter standpoint
they become clearer.

Those who look at the beginnings of the Kingdom as manifested in the life, death, and resurrection of Jesus will see that
the growth of the Kingdom is not a silent, painless process
but a long and painful struggle. The joy of seeing the full
manifestation of the Kingdom comes only to those who have
felt the sting of the crown of thorns. The resurrection and
new life of the Kingdom are attainable only at the end of the
Via Dolorosa. So the planting of the seed will prove to be not
simply a neutral act and a prelude to waiting, but the un-
leashing of something powerful which catches the planter
and those who stand with him powerfully into it.

Striking in the parable of the Kingdom found in Matt.
13:44 is the fact that the treasure (the Kingdom of Heaven)
is already in the field. How it got there is not stated; the

Kingdom is simply a given. Furthermore, there can be no question about the reality or value of the Kingdom. In v. 44 (as in vs. 45–46) it is a thing of such stunning worth that all other treasures pale by comparison.[48] Unlike the parable of the mustard seed, the parable of the buried treasure specifically invites the hearer to go and do something about it. The action of the finder of the treasure is meant to incite the hearer to take similar action. What acquiring the treasure/Kingdom means in terms of the subsequent life-style of the finder is not given. But the treasure is at hand, and the hearer is challenged to make any sacrifice necessary ("selling all that he has") to begin to participate now in the life of the Kingdom. Essentially the same point is made in the ensuing parable of the pearl of great price (13:45–46).

Other parables of the Kingdom, including Matt. 13:24–30 (36–43) and 47–50, make divine judgment and The Retribution their central concerns. Not so the parables of the treasure and the pearl. They do not choose to view the Kingdom as a place of separation of wheat and tares, good and rough fish, sheep and goats. No, above all the Kingdom is a treasure so precious that it must be seized. These parables invite the believer to enter now into the joy and discipline of participation in the Kingdom, although they do not themselves provide details to illustrate the style of Kingdom living. In the broader context of the Gospel, however, they point to a style of living which anticipates the ultimate eschatological universalization of the healing, loving, saving qualities of Jesus' own life and which therefore prefigures the eschatological events of resurrection, gospel proclamation, and the redemption of the whole world.[49] What other style of living would be appropriate to anyone who has in hand the pearl of great price?

Before we leave the topic of the Kingdom of Heaven, it is important that we take another look at the hopes of the New Testament apocalyptic tradition for the full manifestation of the Kingdom. The parables of the Kingdom which we have examined deal primarily with the present, private, and personal response of hearers and believers to the initial event of that Kingdom among men in the person of Jesus. But what will the full growth of the mustard seed imply for those same persons, as well as for nonbelievers? Specifically, does the full advent of the Kingdom require as an essential component the definitive and eternal destruction of all that is imperfect in the creation in a great act of divine Retribution?

My own answer to these questions is this: The ultimately significant claim of the New Testament apocalypse about the full manifestation of the Kingdom is not that divine retribution will be displayed on a cosmic scale against all that has proved inimical to God's redemptive purpose. Rather, his way of tempering his righteous wrath with his saving mercy will be vindicated. Even as Christ's way of dealing with evil was validated through resurrection, so God will vindicate himself more surely with the life of his creation than with its death. In this way will he demonstrate his success at perfecting his redemptive purpose in the cosmos.

A similar point of view was taken some years ago by Mathias Rissi in his concise and original treatment of the book of Revelation, *Time and History*.[50] Rissi finds in the apocalypse four eschatological events, the first being the incarnation. The second event is the resurrection of the martyrs, recounted in Rev. 20:5.[51] The third eschatological event is the general resurrection, final judgment, and second death of Rev. 20:12 ff. Here those who were dead before and during the millennial period are raised and judged, and the wicked are banished to the lake of fire along with Death and Hades. These stages of the drama are quite clear and evident. However, in detecting yet a fourth eschatological event in the culminating chapters of Revelation, Rissi's thinking moves sharply away from that of many other interpreters. This fourth event is yet another resurrection and the "redemption of those who [from the time of the second death] have suffered under God's wrathful eschatological judgment."[52]

This final resurrection is not specifically mentioned in Revelation, as Rissi acknowledges, but can be presumed after 20:6. On what basis? One must refer back to an earlier New Testament use of the normal apocalyptic scenario in I Cor. 15: 22 f., where this fourth event can be found, precisely in the word *telos,* "the end" or "the rest" (v. 24).[53] With the help of this Pauline insight, Rev., ch. 21, then takes on dramatic new scope. In 21:24 ff. the gates of the New Jerusalem stand open onto the only other entity remaining after the Eschaton, the lake of fire; and through these gates flow the "kings of the earth." This term is used elsewhere to denote the enemies of Christ. For Rissi, then, the ultimate end foreseen in Revelation is one in which a walled New Jerusalem, standing in the midst of the lake of fire, opens its gates to receive all those who had suffered for a time, *but not eternally,* the pangs of God's wrath.

Although the difficulties of this argument can be pointed out,[54] it has the merit of taking seriously not only features of the text (and the relation of those features to New Testament apocalyptic elements evidenced elsewhere), but also the larger Biblical motifs of retribution—God's offense at evil and power to extirpate it; and redemption—God's intention to perfect his creation and power to do so. It contends that the Christian apocalyptist, like Paul before him, was a "universalist." This is not the universalism known in modern liberal doctrinal theology, a universalism arrived at by logical arguments. Instead, it is implicit in the received apocalyptic tradition itself. It is a vision which can see, beyond the consuming lake of fire which embodies God's retributive seriousness against evil and burns up all accomplishments that are evil (see I Cor. 3:13–15), the ultimate victory of the Redeemer God in the full manifestation of the Kingdom of Heaven. If Rissi is right, the final act of the drama of redemption, which takes place even beyond The Retribution, is the welcoming of all creation back into the New Jerusalem, where the curses against Adam and Babel are at last overcome, and "God [is] everything to every one" (I Cor. 15:28).

From the beginning of this book I have attempted to show the profound interrelationship of the Biblical motifs of divine retribution and the divine purpose of redemption for both individuals and the cosmos. I have also proposed that the second motif ultimately encompasses and comprehends the former. This is the arrangement which I believe the Christological center of the Scriptures demands. It indicates the priority of redemption over retribution, though not to the exclusion of the latter, which I believe the overall structure of the Bible presupposes. Within that dramatic structure, beginning with the fall of Adam and his expulsion from Paradise, the people of faith have sought to find the way back through the open gates of the New Jerusalem. Now the latest writer of the Bible, and, as an apocalyptist, one of those most seriously committed to affirming God's retributive power even on a cosmic scale, affirms that those gates are open to the very "kings of the earth." Surely, then, the thesis has support. Surely the architecture of the Biblical narrative is itself a demonstration of the conviction that God's redemptive scheme includes and ultimately supersedes his commitment to achieve perfect justice through retribution.

Direction

By way of summarizing this final examination of Biblical texts which check and correct the powerful retributional motif in Scripture, I should like to advance yet another short series of interpretive principles. First of all, I would repeat my earlier contention that (1) *as a detailed account of factual matters regarding the future of the universe, the grand apocalyptic scenario is of no value.*[55] This is simply to say that the details of time, place, numbers, beasts, darkened sun and moon, rapture, earthquakes, gathering at Zion, trumpets, angels, and all the rest belong to the colorful language of the apocalyptic literary genre but are in no way able to set forth in advance the actual course of events. It follows, then, that (2) *the value of the apocalyptic tradition for Christian preaching and believing hinges on assessing the full thrust of the Biblical apocalyptic tradition, rather than simply a study of its parts.* This cuts against proof-texting from Daniel and Revelation, on the ground that no detailed element makes adequate sense apart from the whole picture. (3) *The key factors in that thrust are: (a) the vindication of God's way of dealing with the world and the evil in it; and (b) the invitation to persons of goodwill to live as participants in the Kingdom of Heaven.* By way of further elucidation of this third thesis, I would add that "vindication" involves the unmasking and overcoming of evil, and the perfecting of the creation in all its parts. Whether in Danielic, gospel, Pauline, or Johannine apocalyptic modes of expression, the eschatological texts foresee a manifestation of evil in some palpable form, its defeat, and the ensuing establishment of God's Kingdom. In these acts God's power to carry off his full purpose is made evident. He is vindicated.

Furthermore, the unmasking and overcoming of evil need not, indeed, should not, be expressed simply in terms of divine retribution. This victory of God can be ultimately expressed in terms of divine redemption (I Cor. 15:28). God is shown to be king even over Hades and Death precisely when he liberates and redeems the world from the worst they can do. The practical implication of this for Christian living, as already suggested by the parables of the Kingdom cited above, is this. By being invited to live now as participants in the Kingdom of Heaven, people are inspired by the daily intervention of prayer and the imitation of Christ in their living with others, rather than by the possibility of a single remote divine intervention.

Chapter V

TOWARD
A NON-RETRIBUTIONAL
LIFE-STYLE

The review of Biblical materials is now complete. Whether or not the study has made a contribution remains to be tested in the lives of people. Will this exercise in Biblical theology turn out also to be an exercise in practical theology? Will it make us more sensitive toward the fears and hopes of those we seek to assist in finding a more mature faith? If so, the exercise has succeeded; if not, it has failed.

The problem has been the Biblical imagery of God as re-tributor, as the one who rewards and—most especially—punishes. So often that problem appears in the form of the perennial question of the human sufferer, "Why is God doing this to me?" In the play *The Member of the Wedding,* Carson McCullers tells the story of a twelve-year-old girl who faces the awful prospect of losing her beloved brother to another woman through marriage. The young girl is in despair at how to handle this new fact in her life. Finally she reaches the decision to accompany the newlyweds on their honeymoon. Needless to say, this solution to her problem does not work out. Only through the sensitivity and compassion of the hero-ine of the play, the black housekeeper, Berenice Sadie Brown, is the young girl kept from falling to pieces in the face of this apparent rejection. The play ends ironically: the twelve-year-old gets things back together again, evidently by becoming thirteen, but life falls to pieces for the housekeeper who saved the day. Berenice's brother is caught in a fracas and ultimately hangs himself in jail, and the little cousin of the twelve-year-old, a beloved child who was always very much a part of the daily life of Berenice Sadie Brown, dies of meningitis. The confused woman can only confess, "Looks like a judgment on me." Later she limply says, "I just don't know what I have done to deserve it."

One longs to cry out, "No, no, Berenice Sadie Brown! Don't say it is a judgment. Don't say, 'I just don't know what I've done to deserve it.' Don't ever think that God did something to you. That is the wrong way to state the problem. Putting the problem that way inevitably leads to the wrong answer."

But how does one set up the problem correctly? Surely that cry, "Looks like a judgment on me!" is a cry deeply rooted in the Bible and couched in the language of religion. Therefore, Bible and religion have the obligation to respond to it. If Biblical theology can help people so that they know what to think and say when they suffer pain or bereavement, or experience unjust punishment, then it can make a contribution of major importance to the human condition!

Our task is to join with human sufferers in thinking through the problem of divine retribution and the proportionality between love and justice in God's dealing with his people. From the very foreword of this book, I have tried to be clear about the position from which I begin as a person and believer. My own initial response to the retributional question, "Why is God doing this to me?" is always going to be simple: "God isn't doing this to me. I may be doing something to myself, others may be doing something to me, or it may be by pure chance. But, I don't blame God for this; he does not act in this way!" However, I have also sought to transcend my own starting point. How can those for whom the question is so crucial find an answer grounded in faith? How does the Bible address the matter of divine reward-and-punishment, curse-and-blessing, redemption and retribution? To explore that question is to lay a groundwork upon

which a truly satisfying Biblical and then theological response to the human fear of judgment can be offered.

The method of this study has required two great cycles
through the literature of the Bible. In the first cycle I surveyed a number of texts which developed the motif of divine
retribution in one way or another. In the *lex talionis* we saw
a secular, legal form of this principle of retaliation for evil
committed. We saw historical applications of the idea in the
prophets and in Deuteronomy. In the wisdom psalms, the
Psalms of the Two Ways, we encountered perhaps the clear-
est statement of the principle: God rewards the righteous
and destroys the wicked. In the process of this cycle through
texts which deal with the retributional motif, we also saw
that scholars perceive within the very same texts legitimate
ways of reducing the harshest aspects of the retributional
motif and of opening those texts outward toward a more
inclusive theological framework. For example, some argued
that the suzerainty treaty pattern of covenant formulation,
with its sanctions of curse and blessing so closely associated
with the theme of divine retribution, is not as early as had
formerly been thought.[1] This would mean that the formal
element of curse-and-blessing would not necessarily typify
Israel's way of thinking about Yahweh's response to human
behavior until possibly even as late as the Deuteronomic
period. Another way of blunting the harshest aspect of the
divine retribution scheme was presented in the thought of
Klaus Koch.[2] For Koch, the Bible generally intends to affirm
that human deeds produce their own necessary and inexorable destinies; therefore, God is not involved in the retributional process at all.

Yet another approach intended to reduce the simple
retributional impact of certain texts, particularly in
Deuteronomy, suggested that such texts really are outlining
the probationary and pedagogical activity of God and are
therefore designed to interpret suffering as a means of creat-
ing character.[3] Theodicy was the rubric under which yet

other approaches to retributional materials sought to overcome the simple "suffering is divine punishment" motif.[4]
According to this view, the real purpose in God's wrathful
activity, particularly in end-times, is to vindicate himself. It
is not so much to burn up all the stubble and trash of the
world as it is to show that he is God and that he is able to bring
his history to the fulfillment of his own choosing. Finally, the
very literary form of the book of Deuteronomy seemed to me
suggestive of a way of giving a softening nuance to the obvious retributional understanding of history contained in the
book.[5] Israel is left at the brink of the Jordan not yet fore-
sworn to a course that will lead to certain disaster.
Deuteronomy, and the Deuteronomic history written under
its influence, profoundly believes and teaches the axiom "If
you obey, you will be rewarded, but if you do not, all these
curses will come upon you." The ultimate invocation of the
curse against Israel, however, is never recorded. The people
wait eternally at the bank of the Jordan. In the open-ended
literary structure of the book, the people still have the option
to obey. In its form and in its hortatory style, the book
emerges as an evangelical appeal to obedience rather than
an announcement of doom.

These limitations and caveats upon the motif of divine
retribution, in the very texts which make heaviest use of it,
do not, however, add up to an overcoming of the doctrine.
No, they do not. The notion that God punishes evildoers and
rewards those who love him and keep his commandments is
simply too integral to Scripture to be glossed over or alleged
to be absent. The idea is there; the idea of a day of reckoning
is there; the idea that evil deeds do not lead to life but to
death is there. The theme must be reckoned as a significant
witness to the Word of God. The extent to which this significant Biblical motif (especially in its eschatological form) ex-
erts power in systematic theology was amply illustrated in a
review of confessional statements in Chapter III.

It is my thesis, however, that the theme of divine retribu-

tion is not simply balanced by a corresponding and countervailing motif of the divine intention to redeem the world, but
is actually embraced and comprehended by it. The effort to
sustain that argument occupied our attention in a second
cycle through the Scriptures in Chapter IV. My contention
was that the comprehension of the retribution motif within
the redemption framework was not a quantitative matter.
The Deuteronomic corpus alone is massive and forms the
core of the Bible's theological interpretation of experience in
the categories of reward and punishment. To it must be
added strong elements of the prophetic canon, the Psalter,
and the apocalyptic literature. To put it simply, more Biblical
texts talk about God as the retributor than talk about him as
redeemer. However, such a quantitative evaluation of the
relative priority of the two ways of understanding God's response to human striving would be a wrong approach in any
case.

My approach is instead a structural one. I have argued for
the primacy of the redemption scheme on the basis of what
I have occasionally called the "architecture" of the Bible.
Here is a book that begins with Eden and ends with a New
Jerusalem that bears all the hallmarks of paradise restored.
Here is a book which has at its very center a keystone upon
which the entire structure depends. That balance point I
have otherwise identified as the Christological center. The
Biblical theological claim which, for Christians, stands above
every other claim, is the norm against which every other
teaching and motif has to be measured. That architecture,
having that beginning and that end and that keystone in the
middle, visibly surrounds the massive Biblical theme of divine retribution with an edifice of world redemption and
salvation. If this is indeed so, then perhaps we are on sound
ground in suggesting that the Bible itself seeks to affirm that
God's love and saving power ultimately encompass and comprehend his wrath and retributive justice. The metaphor of
the Biblical drama of redemption serves to convey the same

argument. The drama stretches from the beginning at the Garden of Eden which was the spiritual home of all *ādām;* to the resurrection in the middle, which is the vindication of one *ādām* that bespeaks healing and hope, new life and reconciliation, forgiveness and redemption, for all *ādām;* to the final act in which all *ādām* find their way through fire into the city that is their ultimate home.

The second cycle through the Scriptures seeks to show the validity of this proposed juxtaposition of the motifs of retribution and redemption by examining texts which were themselves similarly juxtaposed to those which were examined on the first cycle. Over against the *lex talionis* and Deuteronomy, I looked at the J creation story in Genesis. In contrast to the prophetic oracles of judgment, I examined the prophetic promise. Job and Ecclesiastes countered the language of the Psalms of the Two Ways. Christological materials and parables of the Kingdom were examined as alternatives to the apocalyptic world judgment by God and the Son of Man.

By way of summary and conclusion at the end of this survey I would offer several observations. (1) The several stages of the Biblical redemption motif, when set alongside the several stages of the Biblical retribution motif, prove to be not only an alternative to the latter but also a greater context for it. We cannot say, then, that the *lex talionis* or even a fixed pattern of reward and punishment is the normative Biblical formulation of God's response to human activity. (2) Evil exists. It must be taken as seriously as God took it on the cross. It must be fought with moral, spiritual, and even physical force. (3) Death exists. It too must be taken seriously and agonized over as deeply as did the one who cried, "My God, my God, why hast thou forsaken me?" It must be seen for what it is, a challenge to the right of any person to continue in existence. Nothing in our studies warrants our saying in the face of death, in some cozy, parental sort of way, "Everything is going to be all right." No, even old age should "burn

and rage at close of day." So the vision of the ultimate triumph of God's redeeming power rendered to us in the Bible
is not an invitation to accept cheap grace and flaccid opti-
mism. (4) From these studies it follows that the relationship
of suffering and death to evil and sin is ambiguous. Within the
Bible itself the two are not always inevitably and predictably
linked. Not all Biblical writers say: "So you sinned! Be prepared for God's punishment!" Some lead the way for us toward what I believe to be the absolutely crucial Christian
affirmation that suffering and even death are best viewed as
essentially secular events. They are events which occur
within the larger sphere of God's providence (the sphere of
his "allowable" will). They are directly attributable not to his
judging activity but quite often to discernible and mundane
cause-and-effect sequences. Seldom, if ever, have we any
reason to say, "God took my loved one to be with him" (much
less, "See how God deals with his enemies!"), and the Bible
will support our refusal to say it. To the mourning parents of
a deceased child, some non-retributional texts (especially Job
and Ecclesiastes) will affirm the true inexplicability of tragedy, while others (the creation stories, Jesus' teaching, eschatological texts) will affirm the promise that death, evil,
and the decay of the world we know shall be overcome.
From the perspective of this faith, one is enabled to look at
essentially secular events and discover in them occasions
wherein "the works of God might be made manifest" (John
9:3). The events, however, remain essentially secular.

One of the great advances of Biblical studies and theology
of our own time has been the affirmation of the place and
integrity of the secular world within the life of faith. To the
secular aspect of our experience, for example, belong the
cause-and-effect sequences set in motion by human willful-
ness or negligence. To see any divine intervention in such
sequences is to obscure the facts, and to run the risk of having
to affirm that every accident or crime or stupidity happens
because God wills it. Scripture itself, of course, sometimes

moves in this direction ("even the hairs of your head are all numbered," Matt. 10:30). In fact, texts which incorporate the retributional motif tend strongly in that direction. But, more astonishingly and more importantly for our purposes, Scripture also warrants our affirmation of what we know to be the case, namely, that there are events in the world which happen by chance or because some chain of causes made them inevitable, and over which God exercises sovereignty only in the remote sense of allowing them to take place within his created world. Included in that sphere in which God does not exercise sovereignty is our human freedom to say "yes" or "no" to him.

The Biblical faith gives us both a basis for making redemptive interpretations of events and spiritual power to cope with them, even though the secular character of the events themselves must be kept very clear. We can interpret secular events in the twin terms of retribution, which takes evil so seriously, and redemption, which surrounds and overcomes retribution, and so begin to lend theological sense to what happens to us. From that point it may even fall out that our faith can direct us toward making significant alterations in the sequences of events which impinge upon us. It is through this agency of obedient and religiously sensitive persons who are led to bring his will to bear on secular causes and effects that God's redemptive purpose is carried forward in the world.

An application of the modern concept of the "secular" to the Biblical drama is suggestive. One might argue that the garden at the beginning was a place of innocence because the secular and the sacred were perceived as one and the same. In Eden all that happened took place under the direct aegis and agency of God. In the mythic drama of the Fall, sin inaugurated the secular sequence of causes and effects which is in a broken and separated relationship to God's will. The very existence of that sequence is a token of the reality of sin. Secular history will retain its own direction until God brings it once again under his own direct aegis at that eschatological moment when he becomes "everything to every one." We live in the intermediate period during which all kinds of things happen to us apart from the will of God and quite independently of his agency. It is because of this that the relationship of sin to suffering remains ambiguous. Were our lives not firmly rooted in the cause-and-effect sequences of secular history, the relationship would be direct. As things stand, however, our acts function as "destiny-producing deeds" which culminate sometimes in joy and sometimes in disaster.

John 3:16 ff. suggested to us that since the Fall all persons lived and moved in a world quite devoid of the possibility of right praxis or perception. John called that world "darkness" (3:19). Once we confront the Christ and recognize in him the Redeemer, we can grow up in the faith (John's "light"), though our daily lives and deeds continue to be played out in the secular world. Now, however, we can interpret, cope, and even allow what happens to us secularly to occasion responses in us that are congruent with life in the Kingdom. Insofar as we can participate authentically in the life of faith and through it make sense of the secular joys, suffering, and death which we undergo, we are living proleptically. We are overcoming the sting of secularity by our participation in the Kingdom of Heaven, even though we do not pretend that the two aspects of our experience are really one and the same.

I now return to my summary remarks with two final observations. (5) Attempts to build a personal life-style upon premises based upon God's transcendent attributes, his perfect justice, perfect power, and omnipresence, will fail. This was Job's discovery. We do logically and rightly acknowledge his perfect justice, and yet injustice abounds. We can and must acknowledge his omnipotence, and yet our weakness and failure are manifest in spite of our pleas for help. Biblical realism and the incarnation itself show us that, in fact, our life-styles as Christians have to be built upon the knowledge that God is *pro nobis*. He is with us in our lives of faith, he is for us in our secular lives, he is Immanuel. We cannot assume that his perfect justice or power will solve our problems when secular events catch up with us, but we can assume that he will not abandon us. To a human sufferer who is tempted to blame the omnipotent God for his own tragedy, the focus on "God with us" can come as cause for hope and joy.

(6) Yet one more observation drawn from these studies is this: If the goal of the world is its redemption, then the same must apply in the cosmic dimensions of creation. Although the freedom of persons to choose to be and to remain incompatible with God is assumed even by our most recent confessions of faith, the hypothesis of an eternal hell must be seen as an affront to God's ability to complete his purpose. In great measure hell arose as a logical necessity, once the retribution motif was projected into the cosmic dimension. But if divine retribution, even in its cosmic and eschatological form, is set in the larger environment of an eschatological triumph of God's plan of salvation, then hell loses its significance. The Bible itself does not solve all the problems on this matter. Our struggles with I Cor. 15:20–28 and Rev. 20:1 to 21:27 and with the relation of both of them to Jesus' self-understanding of his role as eschatological judge well illustrate that point. The task of Christians is cut out for us in this. Through prayer and disciplined reflection, let us see what more we can learn from the Bible and through the Spirit about the eternal "yes." In the meantime, we can embrace what Jesus has done for us now and, in service and in joy, enter into his Kingdom while we await the last act.

I would like to conclude by attempting to respond at last to the persons pictured in the four little vignettes with which I began. In this way I hope succinctly to illustrate the practical side of this exercise in Biblical theology. To the confused and guilty father of James,[6] I would respond this way: "To establish norms, to enforce sanctions, to exhibit wrath, is in no way incompatible with the redemptive purpose of God. But this must be done with confidence in a Christ-given destiny for both the problem child and the angry parent. Discipline, human or divine, is not a synonym for furious retaliation; nor is the purpose of law to 'set up' someone to be punished. Wrath and punishment can be righteous if exercised in an environment that is redemptive." To these things the very structure of the Bible bears witness, with its profound interrelating of retribution and redemption and its comprehension of the former in the latter.

To the neo-fundamentalist college girl[7] I would say: "Relax! The world was created good and the people in it are already redeemed and are now awaiting the glad word of their redemption. As a Christian you are free to live gladly in the world along with them. If you recognize that the battle with evil and unbelief goes on everywhere and within everyone, you can rejoice at even the halfhearted affirmations of Jesus' Lordship which you hear from others, and you can encourage them appropriately. You are also free to admit that which you already suspect in your heart, that all personifications of evil as Satan, all descriptions of hell as a lake of fire, all the dramatic canvases on which the picture of the Judgment Day is painted are expressed in symbolic language. Although they point to the serious possibility of deep incompatibility arising between the creatures of this earth and their Creator, that possibility has itself to be seen within the larger, Biblically described possibility of the reconciliation of all things to the Father and the redemption of the whole creation." To these things both the beginning and the end of Scripture bear witness, each in their own way. The apocalyptic scenario is understood not as a projective historical account, but as a literature which conveys both the seriousness of God's struggle with evil and the assurance of his victory.

To Lucy, the youthful and guilty sufferer of venereal disease, and her troubled mother,[8] I would, on the basis of the directions outlined in this study, try to respond as follows:

"Of course God didn't do it to you. The germs did it. The experience is a secular one. Though the sequence of cause-and-effect is involved, neither the cause nor the effect is an act of God. You will suffer physical and emotional pain; perhaps you will grow. Perhaps in time you will put it all behind you. But be sure of this: In all of your ordeal, whether you know it or not, God will be with you, for he is Immanuel. When you can forgive yourself he will be wanting to forgive you, too, for he wants you and your lover and your loved ones and your children yet unborn to be compatible with him and thus part of the world that is being resurrected." To these things Job and the gospel bear witness, offering a possibility of interpretation and future hope greater than that scheme of retributive justice (echoing the language of Deuteronomy and the Psalms of the Two Ways) which the sufferer offers herself.

To Sam Slaytor, the Beirut missionary,[9] I would gladly respond: "The zeal for mission today lies in sharing the news of redemption, the redemption which is accomplished in the death and resurrection which has happened once, for all. The zeal for mission today lies in the opportunity to invite everyone to embrace his or her own redemption, with its discipline, its cross, its joy, and its hope. Accompanying this word of good news will be deeds that are modern analogies to Jesus' healing miracles, prefigurations of life as it is lived in the Kingdom of Heaven. But to spend time consigning the unevangelized to hell on the basis of arguments from particular Biblical texts is not an adequate basis for missionary zeal." To such a statement the teachings of Jesus, including some of the parables of the Kingdom, bear witness. So, too, do his death, resurrection and all that gives Christians the confidence that in him the Kingdom of Heaven is inaugurated already.

In the light of all that has been concluded, I must address a final word to the question of prayer. Recently I heard a

declamation of Henry van Dyke's not-so-well known story
"The Lost Word." This story tells about a pagan citizen of
Antioch who had become a Christian under the influence of
St. John Chrysostom, only to revert again to his former religion through the manipulations of a pagan priest at a shrine
of Apollo. The priest had asked for the young man's Christian
faith in exchange for wealth, prosperity, and a beautiful wife.
The exchange was made, and the young man attained his
riches, his wife, and a lovely child. But, he could no longer
remember a thing about the Christian faith, not even the
name of Jesus. The inevitable happened. The fair boy was
injured in a chariot accident, and lay dying. The parents tried
desperately to save him. They prayed—but they could not
remember the name to whom the prayer could be addressed. In the nick of time, St. John Chrysostom arrived,
drove off the lurking priest of Apollo, and gave his former
disciple once again the name of Jesus. The couple asked that
their sins be forgiven. In their ultimate spirit of humble repentance and sincere belief, their prayer was answered. The
child, of course, was then healed.

The story does not ring true, not in the light of these
studies of the retributive and redemptive activity of God as
revealed in Scripture. But what would I do, were I in the
pagan's shoes? If my child lay dying, his skull broken against
a wall, what kind of prayer would I offer? Would I impute the
deed to God as retribution for the sins of my wife and me,
and ask forgiveness for us that our child might be healed? Or
would the prayer go something like this? "O God, you know
what we want, and how desperately we want it. Only you
know whether or how this can be achieved. Show us what,
if anything, we can do. And as for our sins, we ask your
forgiveness, praying that the scales may fall from our eyes, so
that we can feel more deeply the exquisite tenderness of the
love of the child, the searching depth of our married relationship, and the hush of your presence.

"We thank you, O God, that you have put us in a world

which moves within an intricate web of dependable and stable principles, even the principles which determine whether our bodies will live or die. Any other kind of world would be impossible to live in. Help us to strike a harmony with those principles in the midst of which we live so that we will not be living at cross purposes to you.

"We thank you for your presence in trouble and in happiness, and ask for the courage to live for you and, when the time comes, to yield up our lives in the hope and certainty of further living with you."

Such a prayer acknowledges that the possible death of the child would be an essentially tragic, secular event, so that I might not be tempted to construe it as divine punishment or retribution. It would keep the secular sphere of cause-and-effect and the sphere of religious faith and perceptivity carefully separated, so that I might not pretend to think that somehow by my prayers I can cause a brain that has been crushed to become whole again. It would keep me ready to say with a whole heart, "If a way to rebuild the broken body can be found, let us do all we can in that way. But let us also thank God for the dependability of a world in which if our brain is crushed, we die!"

I conclude this study with a speech from the judgment scene in Dorothy Sayers' modern version of the Faustus legend, *The Devil to Pay*. The themes of my book are all caught up here: the integrity of cause-and-effect sequences, the reality of judgment, the centrality of Christ in relating judgment to salvation, and the joyous certainty that divine retribution is finally compassed about by God's redemptive power.

> All things God can do, but this thing He will not:
> Unbind the chain of cause and consequence,
> Or speed time's arrow backward. When man chose
> To know like God, he also chose to be
> Judged by God's values. Adam sinned, indeed,

And with him all mankind; and from that sin
God wrought a nobler virtue out for Adam,
And with him, all mankind. No soul can 'scape
That universal kinship and remain
Human—no man; not even God made man.
He, when He hung upon the fatal tree,
Felt all the passion of the world pierce through Him,
Nor shirked one moment of the ineluctable
Load of the years; but from the griefs of time
Wrought out the splendour of His eternity.
There is no waste with God; He cancels nothing
But redeems all.[10]

NOTES

CHAPTER I.
THE PASTORAL PROBLEM OF PUNISHMENT

1. Out of a variety of terms that might be suitable to characterize an ongoing, complex, and often subtly expressed idea such as "divine retribution," I have selected the term "motif." A "motif" is, according to the *New English Dictionary* (Oxford University Press, 1908), "a type of incident, a particular situation, an ethical problem, or the like, which may be treated in a work of imagination." Although the term sometimes has the more technical sense of a nuance or idea constantly alluded to by a writer for literary effect, I nevertheless find it more suitable as a designation for the frequently raised but often amorphous Biblical issue of divine retribution than "theme," "concept," or "doctrine."

2. So *The Random House Dictionary of the English Language* (Random House, Inc., 1966). For further discussion of the semantics of retribution in the Bible see the Glossary. See my article on "Retribution" in *The Interpreter's Dictionary of the Bible—Supplementary Volume* (Abingdon Press, 1976).

CHAPTER II.
THE DIVINE "NO" IN THE BIBLE

1. This text is more than a mere citation, of course, but provides the *lex talionis* with an extensive interpretation. The process of interpretation, though not the actual Old Testament citation, is

visible elsewhere in Luke 6:29–30; Rom. 12:17–21; I Peter 3:9.

2. Towner, "Retribution," *loc. cit.*

3. See the Glossary for distinctions between the several English terms that might be employed here.

4. The exact meaning of *p^elilim* (v. 22), rendered by RSV as "judges," is disputed. See Martin Noth, *Exodus: A Commentary*, tr. by J. S. Bowden (The Westminster Press, 1962), p. 181; Brevard S. Childs, *The Book of Exodus* (The Westminster Press, 1974), p. 448, n. 22.

5. James B. Pritchard, ed., *Ancient Near Eastern Texts Relating to the Old Testament, with Supplement*, 3d ed. (Princeton University Press, 1969), p. 175. The laws cited here are numbered 195–197, 200, 209–210.

6. G. R. Driver and John C. Miles, *The Assyrian Laws* (Oxford: Clarendon Press, 1935), p. 419. Also translated in Pritchard, *op. cit.*, p. 184.

7. See Sayed Kotb, *Social Justice in Islam* (Washington, D.C.: American Council of Learned Societies, 1953), pp. 66–67; Majid Khadduri and Herbert J. Liebesny, eds., *Law in the Middle East* (Washington, D.C.: Middle East Institute, 1955), Vol. I, pp. 224 ff.

8. See Dorothea C. Leighton and Clyde Kluckhohn, *Children of the People* (Harvard University Press, 1947), p. 171.

9. Ex. 21:36 seems to be a weak application of the principle, but applies to property, not human injuries. Other applications suggested, none of which is entirely convincing for a variety of reasons, include Gen. 9:6; Ex. 32:20; Num. 5:21–22; Deut. 25:11–12; II Sam. 4:12; II Kings 9:26; Dan. 6:24. A classic Pentateuchal statement of the principle of divine reward-and-punishment along distributory, if not strictly retaliatory, lines is Ex. 20:4–6.

10. For other instances of divine application of the law of retaliation, see Jer. 17:10; 50:15; Ezek. 7:8; Obad. 15, *inter alia.*

11. Babylonian Talmud, Baba Kamma 84a.

12. Noth, *op. cit.*

13. Childs, *op. cit.*

14. B. S. Jackson, "The Problem of Exod. XXI 22–5 (Ius talionis)," *Vetus Testamentum*, Vol. XXIII (1973), pp. 273–304.

15. A. S. Diamond, *Primitive Law Past and Present* (Longmans, Green & Company, 1971) and in other works cited by Jackson, *op. cit.*, p. 297, argued that a movement toward the more idealistic

talionic formula away from pecuniary sanctions was a universal phenomenon. The evidence seems to be drawn largely from Western cultures, however.

16. Jackson, *op. cit.*, p. 298.

17. H.-W. Wolff, "Hoseas geistige Heimat," *Theologische Literaturzeitung*, Vol. LXXXI (1956), pp. 83–94, reprinted in his *Gesammelte Studien zum Alten Testament* (Munich: Chr. Kaiser Verlag, 1964), pp. 232–250.

18. H.-W. Wolff, *Hosea*, tr. by Gary Stansell (Fortress Press, 1974), p. xxxi. James L. Mays, *Hosea: A Commentary* (The Westminster Press, 1969), while not endorsing Wolff's theory of the Levitical background of Hosea, is willing to postulate a direct link between Hosea's own immediate circle and later Judean religious groups. See pp. 5, 16.

19. For a very recent review of the form, setting, and scholarly discussion of the "controversy" pattern *(Rīb-Gattung)* of the prophets, see R. E. Clements, *Prophecy and Tradition* (John Knox Press, 1975), pp. 17 ff. See Mays, *op. cit.*, pp. 61–62.

20. A Biblical literary pattern is thought by form critics always to spring from some specific cultural or institutional setting. E. Gerstenberger defines the relationship as follows: A "form of speech" is "a characteristic pattern of language, style, and ideas which is necessitated by concrete and recurring human action in society. Social groups condition and sanction not only the behavior of their members but also their various ways of speaking under given circumstances." See "The Woe-Oracles of the Prophets," *Journal of Biblical Literature*, Vol. LXXXI (1962), p. 249, n. 1.

21. For a fuller development of this "conservative" function of the prophets, see my article "On Calling People 'Prophets' in 1970," *Interpretation*, Vol. XXIV (1970), pp. 492–509.

22. W. Eichrodt, *Theology of the Old Testament*, tr. by J. A. Baker (The Westminster Press, Vol. I, 1961; Vol. II, 1967).

23. Dennis J. McCarthy, S.J., *Treaty and Covenant* (Rome: Pontifical Biblical Institute, 1963), pp. 15–16.

24. See Pritchard, *op. cit.*, pp. 199–206.

25. Following V. Korosec's analysis of the pattern as summarized by George Mendenhall, *Law and Covenant in Israel and the Ancient Near East* (Pittsburgh: The Biblical Colloquium, 1955), pp. 32–34.

26. A developmental sequence similar to the one which I propose here is discussed by Clements, *op. cit.*, pp. 8–23.

27. Ernest W. Nicholson, *Deuteronomy and Tradition* (Fortress Press, 1967), pp. 76 ff.

28. *Ubāhartā* is the Qal perfect second person masculine singular form of the verb *bāhar,* "to choose." With the *waw* consecutive, however, the verb carries an imperfect or even imperative sense, i.e., a sense of not-yet-completed action.

29. In his article "The Theology of Retribution in the Book of Deuteronomy," *Catholic Biblical Quarterly,* Vol. XXXII (1970), pp. 1–12, John G. Gammie proposes that four stages or nuances of retributional theology are discernible within the single book. The fourth stage, which Gammie identifies as the beginning of the dissolution of the scheme of divine retribution, may provide yet other mitigating elements to the otherwise thoroughly consistent reward-and-punishment pattern of the book. Gammie argues, for example, that the pericope Deut. 8:1 to 9:6 invokes interpretations of some of Israel's suffering in the wilderness-wandering period as probationary and pedagogical rather than punitive, and understands Israel's ultimate safety as a gracious gift of Yahweh rather than a merited reward. Gammie further points to Deut. 9:7b to 10:11 as evidence that God can be dissuaded from implementing his retributional penalty by the prayers of a humble man—a possibility which, of course, should be ruled out by a strict understanding of a binding covenant obligation upon Yahweh to reward obedience and punish transgression!

30. S. Mowinckel assigns these psalms to the work of scribes and wise men meditating privately on the themes of the Jewish faith. See his *The Psalms in Israel's Worship,* tr. by D. R. Ap-Thomas (Abingdon Press, 1962), Vol. II, pp. 104 ff. Unlike the rest of the Psalter, the wisdom psalms, in which category he includes Ps. 1, 19B, 34, 37, 49, 78, 105, 106, 111, 112, 127, were not primarily intended for cultic use. He notes (p. 112) that "a favourite subject is the instruction about the destinies of good and evil people . . . and more or less successful attempts at proving that the Jewish dogma of retributive justice holds good. . . . In this way the psalm [of the Two Ways] receives the character of a theodicy: the author seeks to prove that God has acted rightly."

31. M. Dahood, S. J., *Psalms I:1–50. The Anchor Bible* (Doubleday

& Company, Inc., 1965), pp. 1–5. M. Dahood understands the psalm to be dealing throughout with eschatological themes. For him, the "transplanting" of v. 3 is an eschatological transferal of the righteous to the underworld abode of the just. The "tree," "streams of water," and the "judgments" (v. 5) are also to be understood in their eschatological senses. The effect of this understanding is to heighten the retributional content of the psalm and make it correspond to the vision of The Day of Retribution pictured in later Jewish apocalyptic literature. Although I find this interpretation extreme, it certainly does not gainsay the strongly felt presence of the retributional motif in the psalm.

32. H.-J. Kraus, *Psalmen I: Biblischer Kommentar Altes Testament,* 2d ed. (Neukirchen: Neukirchener Verlag, 1961), pp. 1–10.

33. Klaus Koch, "Gibt es ein Vergeltungsdogma im Alten Testament?" *Zeitschrift für Theologie und Kirche,* Vol. LII (1955), pp. 1–42. Reprinted together with responses and additional studies by F. Horst, H. Gese, W. Preiser, J. Scharbert, *et al.,* in K. Koch, ed., *Um das Prinzip der Vergeltung in Religion und Recht des Alten Testaments* (Darmstadt: Wissenschaftliche Buchgesellschaft, 1972).

34. In addition to the essays collected in the volume cited in the previous note, see also Gammie, *op. cit.* Also Gerhard von Rad, *Wisdom in Israel* (London: SCM Press, Ltd., 1972), p. 128, n. 19.

35. James Barr, *The Semantics of Biblical Language* (Oxford University Press, 1961), pp. 50–57 *passim.*

36. The term "mythic" is a technical one. B. S. Childs, *Myth and Reality in the Old Testament,* 2d ed. (London: SCM Press, Ltd., 1962), pp. 29–30, says: "Myth is a form by which the existing structure of reality is understood and maintained. It concerns itself with showing how an action of a deity, conceived of as occurring in the primeval age, determines a phase of contemporary world order." Technically speaking, then, myths are accounts of the beginnings of realities which continue to form a part of our experience and will continue to do so even at the Eschaton. The "mythic" aspects of apocalyptic literature are simply allusions to, expressions of, and reflections upon those divine activities and cosmic realities which were also present at the creation.

37. Stanley B. Frost, *Old Testament Apocalyptic: Its Origins and Growth* (London: The Epworth Press, 1952), pp. 34–39.

38. A similar move from prophetic eschatology toward the images

of recrudescent myth in the development of Old Testament apocalyptic is postulated by Paul D. Hanson, "Old Testament Apocalyptic Reexamined," *Interpretation,* Vol. XXV (1971), pp. 454–479. See pp. 470 ff.

39. *Ibid.,* p. 468. See also Paul D. Hanson, *The Dawn of Apocalyptic* (Fortress Press, 1975), pp. 26 ff., 96, *et passim.*

40. Otto Plöger, *Theocracy and Eschatology,* tr. by S. Rudman (John Knox Press, 1968).

41. Hanson, *Dawn,* concludes his important study with the pessimistic observation that by the time Old Testament apocalyptic reaches the stage represented by Zech., ch. 14, "the powerful ethical consciousness of prophecy . . . has been swallowed up by a morbid preoccupation with the damnation of the oppressor." The apocalyptists tend to "remove themselves further and further from the realities of the community within which [they] live but are not a part" (p. 399). Hanson sees positive implications of Old Testament apocalyptic for theology and ethics which he promises to develop in the future (pp. 409–10). Meanwhile, he appears to find more historical than kerygmatic value in the material.

42. In the interests of space and readability I omit any discussion of intertestamental Jewish apocalyptic literature, even though it must be assumed to reveal stages of development in apocalyptic intervening between Daniel and the book of Revelation.

43. P. Vielhauer, "Apocalyptic in Early Christianity," in E. Hennecke and W. Schneemelcher, eds., *New Testament Apocrypha,* Vol. II, tr. by R. McL. Wilson (The Westminster Press, 1962), p. 616.

44. G. Bornkamm, "Die Komposition der apokalyptischen Visionen in der Offenbarung Johannis," in his *Studien zu Antike und Urchristentum* (Munich: C. Kaiser Verlag, 1959), pp. 204–222. Cited by Vielhauer, *op. cit.,* pp. 621–622.

CHAPTER III. RELATING THE DIVINE "NO"
TO THE DIVINE "YES"

1. Text cited from John H. Leith, ed., *Creeds of the Churches,* rev. ed. (John Knox Press, 1973), p. 73.

2. The Catholic theologian John Eck had, in his *404 Articles* (addressed to the emperor in March, 1530), identified the Lutherans

with the teaching of the Anabaptist Hans Denk that "wicked spirits will hereafter be saved with the damned" (Art. 394). The confession is at pains to dissociate the Lutheran faith from such teaching. See M. Reu, *The Augsburg Confession: A Collection of Sources with an Historical Introduction* (Wartburg Publishing House, 1930), pp. 97–121.

3. John H. Leith, *Assembly at Westminster: Reformed Theology in the Making* (John Knox Press, 1973), p. 21.

4. The same difficulty confronted us in dealing with Rev. 20:12 when we attempted to discern the relation of the heavenly record books to the "book of life." See above, pp. 62–64.

5. The text of this statement is appended to the Confession as it appears in *The Constitution of The United Presbyterian Church in the United States of America, Part I: Book of Confessions,* and is numbered paragraphs 6.176 to 6.178.

6. Harry Buis, *The Doctrine of Eternal Punishment* (Presbyterian and Reformed Publishing Company, 1957).

7. No one treatment can adequately account for the vast literature dealing with the subject of divine retribution from Biblical and patristic times down to the present. Substantial studies of at least segments of the ongoing process of reflection on the theme include James P. Martin, *The Last Judgment in Protestant Theology from Orthodoxy to Ritschl* (Wm. B. Eerdmans Publishing Company, 1963); Leon Morris, *The Biblical Doctrine of Judgment* (London: Tyndale Press, 1960); Geoffrey Rowell, *Hell and the Victorians* (Oxford University Press, 1974); and D. P. Walker, *The Decline of Hell: Seventeenth-Century Discussions of Eternal Punishment* (The University of Chicago Press, 1964). The Rowell book deals in particular with the controversies upon the subject of The Retribution between the high-church Anglicans of the nineteenth century, represented above all by E. B. Pusey, and the broad-church movement represented by F. D. Maurice.

8. Buis, *op. cit.,* p. 2.

9. *Ibid.,* p. 33.

10. *Ibid.,* p. 34.

11. Among the texts which he cites are Matt. 5:22, 29–30; 7:19; 10:28; 11:22–24; 13:40–42; 23:15, 33; 25:41–46.

12. See Rom. 2:3–9, 12; I Cor. 3:17; II Cor. 5:10; I Thess. 5:3. Needless to say, he can cite numerous texts from the other epistles

as well: Heb. 2:2–3; 6:1–2; 10:28–31, 39; II Peter 2:4–9, 12–13a, 17, 21; Jude 6, 7, 13–15.

13. Buis, *op. cit.*, p. 51.

14. *Ibid.*, pp. 135–36.

15. *Ibid.*, pp. 121–22. I have in my file an essay by the columnist Jenkin Lloyd Jones which appeared in the November 9, 1975, issue of the *Richmond Times-Dispatch.* I feel certain he speaks for many when, writing against the recent marked increase in the incidence of terrorist attacks around the world, he invokes the *lex talionis* with these words: "Terrorism is the ultimate 'situational ethics' with which some of our campus luminaries and even churchmen were intrigued in the crazy '60s. . . . But we can't live with it. We will either learn to control terrorism by judicious and selective counter-measures, or we will have the chaos of vigilantism or the ruthless discipline of tyrants.

"Is there any future for humanity if we don't start weeping over the slaughter of the innocent, and demanding an eye for an eye?"

If men ought to retaliate against the wicked of their society with "judicious and selective countermeasures," how much more, in his view, ought God to do so?

16. The point is well illustrated by the somewhat disturbingly effective use of these parables in the rock gospel *Godspell.*

17. For a forthright contemporary exposition of the value and method of interpretation within the context of the canon, see Brevard S. Childs, *Biblical Theology in Crisis* (The Westminster Press, 1970), esp. pp. 91–122.

18. Gerhard von Rad, *Old Testament Theology,* tr. by D. M. G. Stalker (Harper & Row, Publishers, Inc., Vol. I, 1962; Vol. II, 1965).

19. Eichrodt, *op. cit.*

20. This entire issue of the use of Scripture by theology has recently been fruitfully explored by David H. Kelsey, *The Uses of Scripture in Recent Theology* (Fortress Press, 1975). See esp. pp. 158 ff.

21. See also II Thess. 1:8–9, which speaks both of the "destruction" and the "exclusion" of "those who do not know God."

22. See *The Proposed Book of Confessions of the Presbyterian Church in the United States Together with Related Documents Comprising The Report of The Ad Interim Committee on a New Confession of Faith Together with a Book of Confessions to the*

116th General Assembly of the Presbyterian Church, U.S. (Atlanta: Materials Distribution Service, 1976), p. 253. An earlier study document entitled "A Study of Universalism" (received by the 1974 PCUS General Assembly) appears to be a fuller statement of a similar position, with a more noticeable tilt toward the thesis also espoused by this book, namely, that the Biblical data themselves ultimately warrant the subordination of the retributional motif to the theological assurance of God's purpose ultimately to redeem his entire creation.

23. Emil Brunner, *Eternal Hope,* tr. by Harold Knight (The Westminster Press, 1954), p. 182.

CHAPTER IV. THE DIVINE "YES" AS CONTEXT FOR THE DIVINE "NO"

1. Gerhard von Rad, "The Form-Critical Problem of the Hexateuch," in *The Problem of the Hexateuch and Other Essays,* tr. by E. W. Trueman Dicken (McGraw-Hill Book Co., Inc., 1966), pp. 1–78, esp. pp. 63–67. See also his *Old Testament Theology,* Vol. I, pp. 136–165.

2. In his earlier work, von Rad insisted that the individual creative hand of the J writer is visible in the way in which the older mythic materials are freely woven into the pre-patriarchal history. See "Form-Critical Problem," pp. 64, 67.

3. For an exploration of the tension between the original intention of the mythic materials of Israel's creation accounts and their present function in the text of Genesis, see Childs, *Myth and Reality in the Old Testament.*

4. For a fascinating account of this tragic closing chapter of the Great Commoner's life see Lawrence W. Levine, *Defender of the Faith* (Oxford University Press, 1965), esp. pp. 350–351.

5. The phrase is borrowed from Joni Mitchell's popular song of 1969, "Woodstock."

6. Von Rad, "Form-Critical Problem," pp. 65 ff. See B. Davie Napier, *From Faith to Faith* (Harper & Brothers, 1955), p. 56.

7. See *inter alia,* Claus Westermann, "The Way of Promise Through the Old Testament," in Bernhard W. Anderson, ed., *The Old Testament and the Christian Faith* (Harper & Row, Publishers,

Inc., 1963), pp. 200–224; Walther Zimmerli, "Promise and Fulfillment," in Claus Westermann, ed., *Essays on Old Testament Hermeneutics,* tr. by James L. Mays (John Knox Press, 1963), pp. 89–122.

8. Napier, *op. cit.,* pp. 56, 60–68.

9. Dietrich Bonhoeffer, *Creation and Fall: A Theological Interpretation of Genesis 1–3* (The Macmillan Company, 1959). See esp. pp. 56–57, 92–96.

10. *Ibid.,* pp. 74–76.

11. See above, pp. 35–41.

12. See Jer. 11:18 to 12:3; 15:10 ff.; 17:14–18; 18:18–23; 20:7–18. Also 4:19–21; 5:3–5; 8:18 to 9:1 (8:23 Hebrew). See John Bright, *Jeremiah. Anchor Bible* (Doubleday & Company, Inc., 1974), pp. lxv-lxvii.

13. Although Mays, *op. cit.,* does not specifically interpret this verse in this way, he does observe that many of the oracles of chs. 9 to 12 would fit into the reign of Hoshea (732–724 B.C.), which began immediately after Tiglath-pileser's punitive incursion into the Northern Kingdom in 733 B.C. and ended just before the final destruction of Samaria.

14. J. Philip Hyatt, *Prophetic Religion* (Abingdon-Cokesbury Press, 1947), p. 101.

15. W. F. Stinespring, "Hosea, Prophet of Doom," *Crozer Quarterly,* Vol. XXVII (1950), pp. 200–207. Many years later he reviewed his position and the subsequent discussion of the entire question in an essay entitled "A Problem of Theological Ethics in Hosea," in J. L. Crenshaw and J. T. Willis, eds., *Essays in Old Testament Ethics* (Ktav Publishing House, Inc., 1974), pp. 133–44.

16. "Hosea, Prophet of Doom," p. 205.

17. One excellent example is provided by the Elihu speeches in the Book of Job (chs. 32 to 37), which have been rejected by scholars for years and which even a recent interpreter such as Marvin Pope, *Job. Anchor Bible,* 3d ed. (Doubleday & Company, Inc., 1973), p. xxvii, can call "diffuse and pretentious . . . pompous and prolix. . . ." Yet precisely these speeches are singled out by another distinguished interpreter as representing the more mature insight of the poet of the dialogues. See Robert Gordis, *The Book of God and Man: A Study of Job* (The University of Chicago Press, 1965), pp. 104–116.

18. See above, pp. 47–52.
19. R. B. Y. Scott, *Proverbs, Ecclesiastes. The Anchor Bible* (Doubleday & Company, Inc., 1965), pp. 202–203.
20. *Ibid.,* p. 222.
21. Rudolf Bultmann, *The Gospel of John: A Commentary,* tr. by G. R. Beasley-Murray, *et al.* (The Westminster Press, 1971), pp. 7–9.
22. *Ibid.,* p. 257.
23. W. G. Kümmel, *Promise and Fulfillment—The Eschatological Message of Jesus,* tr. by Dorothea M. Barton (Alec R. Allenson, Inc., 1957), p. 102.
24. *Ibid.,* p. 154.
25. *Ibid.,* p. 95.
26. *Ibid.,* p. 149.
27. *Ibid.,* p. 153.
28. I make particular reference here to the two essays which were published in German in 1960 and 1962 respectively. They first appeared in English as "The Beginnings of Christian Theology" and "On the Topic of Primitive Christian Apocalyptic," in R. W. Funk, ed., *Journal for Theology and the Church 6: Apocalypticism* (Herder & Herder, Inc., 1969), pp. 17–46, 99–133. They were subsequently reprinted in a collection of Käsemann's own essays entitled *New Testament Questions of Today* (Fortress Press, 1969), pp. 82–107, 108–137.
29. "Beginnings," p. 40 (citing the Funk ed.).
30. *Ibid.,* p. 19.
31. *Ibid.,* p. 43.
32. "Topic," p. 103.
33. *Ibid.,* p. 105.
34. *Ibid.*
35. See above, pp. 84–88.
36. Barth treats the doctrine of election in *Church Dogmatics,* Vol. II, pt. 2, ed. and tr. by G. W. Bromiley, T. F. Torrance, *et al.* (Edinburgh: T. & T. Clark, 1957), pp. 1–506. Throughout this section, he struggles with the tension between the reality of the human rejection of God and the reality of God's eternal decree of election of all mankind. To the same issue he returns at length under the topic of "Reconciliation," *Church Dogmatics,* Vol. IV, pt. 1. For a review of the discussion of Barth's "universalism" since the publication of G. C. Berkouwer's *The Triumph of Grace in the Theology*

of Karl Barth, tr. by Harry R. Boer (Wm. B. Eerdmans Publishing Company, 1956), see Joseph D. Bettis, "Is Karl Barth a Universalist?" *Scottish Journal of Theology,* Vol. XX (1967), pp. 423–436. Bettis' own answer to his question is "No," but the qualifications which must necessarily be attached make it a very weak "No" indeed. Says Bettis (p. 427), "Barth consistently rejects universalism as a doctrine, but he leaves open the possibility that within God's freedom all men may indeed be saved."

37. C. K. Barrett, *A Commentary on the First Epistle to the Corinthians* (Harper & Row, Publishers, Inc., 1968), p. 5.

38. *Ibid.,* p. 353.

39. *Ibid.,* pp. 351–53. Compare the sequence in I Thess. 4:16.

40. A similar synonymous use of *dia* and *en* to refer to the agency or instrumentality of Christ occurs in II Cor. 5:18–19. On the use of *en* to introduce a phrase showing agency or instrumentality, see F. Blass and A. Debrunner, *A Greek Grammar of the New Testament and Other Early Christian Literature,* ed. and tr. by Robert W. Funk (The University of Chicago Press, 1961), par. 219. Other instrumental uses of *en* occur in Matt. 9:34; 12:24.

41. Barrett, *op. cit.,* p. 356.

42. W. F. Arndt and F. W. Gingrich, eds., *A Greek-English Lexicon of the New Testament and Other Early Christian Literature* (The University of Chicago Press, 1957), p. 810.

43. However, strong arguments can be made against the Pauline authorship of II Thessalonians. For a thorough review of the discussion, including his own conclusion in favor of Pauline authorship, see Ernest Best, *A Commentary on the First and Second Epistles to the Thessalonians* (Harper & Row, Publishers, Inc., 1972), pp. 50–58.

44. Oscar Cullmann tries to make a case for a New Testament notion of an intermediate state of the dead in his *Immortality of the Soul or Resurrection of the Dead?* (London: The Epworth Press, 1958). Few others have found the evidence convincing. See the review of the discussion in Karel Hanhart, *The Intermediate State in the New Testament* (Franeker, The Netherlands: T. Wever, 1967).

45. See above, p. 89, and the texts cited there in connection with my treatment of the Confession of 1967, par. 9.11.

46. Proposed Confession, Ch. II, lines 32–35, 1974 ed. The most

recent edition of the Proposed Confession eliminates the last sentence quoted here and substitutes, "In the end evil will be utterly defeated" (II. 42).

47. J. Jeremias, *The Parables of Jesus* (Charles Scribner's Sons, 1955), p. 90.

48. *Ibid.*, p. 140.

49. Obviously I disagree with Kümmel's view (see above, p. 122) that Jesus does not teach that the Kingdom is a present invisible reality in which the believer may participate in the interval between the Passion and the Eschaton. These very parables of the Kingdom seem to be prime evidence against that position. The two in Matt. 13:44–46 in particular seem to be saying nothing if they are not inviting the hearer boldly to attain and to participate in the Kingdom now!

50. Mathias Rissi, *Time and History: A Study on the Revelation* (John Knox Press, 1966). Rissi's position was subsequently spelled out in further detail in his *The Future of the World: An Exegetical Study of Revelation 19:11—22:15* (London: SCM Press, Ltd., 1972).

51. See the earlier treatment of this passage above, pp. 58–67.

52. *Time and History*, p. 124.

53. See the earlier treatment of this passage above, pp. 128–135.

54. The continued apparent reservation in Rev. 21:27 that some are not written in the "Lamb's book of life" poses a problem for this position; a more basic one is posed by the fact that the fourth apocalyptic event is not specifically identified in Revelation and only implicitly in I Cor. 15:24.

55. See above, pp. 58, 65–66, for further discussion.

CHAPTER V.
TOWARD A NON-RETRIBUTIONAL LIFE-STYLE

1. See above, pp. 38 ff.
2. See above, pp. 48 ff.
3. See above, Ch. II, n. 29.
4. See above, Ch. II, n. 30.
5. See above, pp. 44 f.
6. See above, pp. 15–16.
7. See above, pp. 16–18.

8. See above, p. 18.

9. See above, pp. 19–20.

10. Dorothy L. Sayers, *The Devil to Pay* (London: Victor Gollancz, Ltd., 1939), p. 100. Published in Great Britain by Victor Gollancz, Ltd., published in the United States by Vineyard Books, Inc. Used by permission of Victor Gollancz, Ltd.

GLOSSARY

The Biblical motif of divine retribution is far too prevalent, nuanced, and interrelated with other themes to be approachable simply through the study of its typical terminology. However, lexical tools can help locate passages relevant for consideration in a thematic study such as this, and semantic analysis can lend precision to the resulting delineation of the motif in its various forms and settings. As an aid to readers who wish further to pursue the matter of the Biblical motif of divine retribution, I offer here a three-part glossary of English, Hebrew, and Greek terms which bear in varying degrees of importance upon the motif.

ENGLISH NOUNS

(extrapolate to verbal meanings)

judgment	the judicial decision of a cause in court; a misfortune regarded as inflicted by divine sentence, as for sin.
recompense	compensation, as for an injury or wrong; a repayment, requital, or reward for services, favors, etc.
repayment	return, refund.
reprisal	retaliation against an enemy for injuries received by the infliction of equal or greater injuries.
requital	a return or reward for service; a retaliation for wrong, injury, etc.

retaliation	a return of like for like; a reprisal.
retribution	requital according to merits or deserts, esp. (but not exclusively) for evil; the distribution of rewards and punishments in a future life.
revenge	retaliation for injuries or wrongs; vengeance; an opportunity of retaliation or satisfaction.
rewards-and-punishments	recompense for acts performed, services rendered, gifts given, etc. Reward usually implies something given in return for good; punishment always refers to something given in return for evil.
vengeance	infliction of trouble, such as pain, injury, humiliation, or annoyance, on a person or persons who have been a source of injury or annoyance to one.

The following summary of these synonyms taken from *The Random House Dictionary of the English Language,* p. 1226, under the entry for "revenge" will be helpful:

REVENGE, REPRISAL, RETRIBUTION, VENGEANCE suggest a punishment or injury inflicted in return for one received. REVENGE is the carrying out of a bitter desire to injure another for a wrong done to oneself or to those who are felt to be like oneself: *to plot revenge.* REPRISAL, formerly any act of retaliation, is used specifically in warfare for retaliation upon the enemy for his (usually unlawful) actions: *to make a raid in reprisal for one by the enemy.* RETRIBUTION suggests just or deserved punishment, often without personal motives, for some evil done: *a just retribution for wickedness.* VENGEANCE is usually wrathful, vindictive, furious revenge: *implacable vengeance.*

Hebrew Terms

(in alphabetical order by verbal stems)

gāmal	"to recompense, requite"
	nouns: *gᵉmūl, gᵉmūlāh,* "recompense"
nāqam	"to avenge"
	nouns: *nāqām, nᵉqāmāh,* "vengeance"
sākar	"to hire"
	noun: *maskōret,* "wages"
shālēm	"to requite, recompense"
	nouns: *shillēm, shillūm, shillumāh,* "requital"

Greek Terms

(in alphabetical order)

antapodidōmi	"recompense"
antapodoma	"retribution"
antapodosis	"recompense"
apodidōmi	"repay, reward"
dikē	"justice, punishment"
ekdikeō	"avenge"
ekdikēsis	"vengeance"
misthapodosia	"retribution"
misthos	"wages"
orgē	"wrath (of God)"

FOR FURTHER READING

THE BIBLICAL MOTIF OF RETRIBUTION

Crenshaw, James L., "Popular Questioning of the Justice of God in
Ancient Israel. I. A Famine in the Land of Promise. II. Job and
Qoheleth. III. Survival of a Faithful Few: The Doxology of Judgment. IV. Judgment Through Fire," *Zeitschrift für die alttes-
tamentliche Wissenschaft*, Vol. LXXXII (1970), pp. 188–209.

Filson, Floyd V., *St. Paul's Conception of Recompense*. Leipzig:
J. C. Hinrichs, 1931.

Harrelson, Walter, "Vengeance," *The Interpreter's Dictionary of
the Bible IV*. Abingdon Press, 1962. P. 748.

Jackson, William, *The Doctrine of Retribution*. New York: Randolph
& Company, 1876.

Jaeger, Harry J., Jr., "Love Drives Out Fear," *Presbyterian Life*,
Vol. XXV (August, 1972), pp. 12–16—with responses by J. C.
Reid, Arthur Cochrane. An additional response by W. S.
Towner appeared in *A.D.*, Vol. I (September, 1972), p. 90.

Johnson, S. L., Jr., "God Gave Them Up: A Study in Divine Retribution (Rom. 1:24)," *Bibliotheca Sacra*, Vol. CXXIX (1972), pp.
124–133.

Koch, Klaus, "Gibt es ein Vergeltungsdogma im Alten Testament?"
Zeitschrift für Theologie und Kirche, Vol. LII (1955), pp. 1–42.

——— (ed.), *Um das Prinzip der Vergeltung in Religion und Recht
des Alten Testaments*. Darmstadt: Wissenschaftliche Buchgesellschaft, 1972. (Collected essays on "retribution" in the Old
Testament, including the Koch essay listed above.)

Kümmel, W. G., *Promise and Fulfillment—The Eschatological Mes-*

sage of Jesus, tr. by Dorothea M. Barton. Alec R. Allenson, Inc., 1957.

Lanczkowski, G., Horst, F., *et al.,* "Vergeltung," *Religion in Geschichte und Gegenwart,* Vol. VI (3d ed.), 1962), cols. 1341–1355.

McKeating, Henry, "Vengeance Is Mine: A Study of the Pursuit of Vengeance in the Old Testament," *Expository Times,* Vol. LIV (1963), pp. 239–245.

Mendenhall, George, "The 'Vengeance' of Yahweh," in *The Tenth Generation.* The Johns Hopkins Press, 1973. Pp. 69–104.

Minear, Paul S., *And Great Shall Be Your Reward.* Yale University Press, 1941.

Paul, R. S., *Kingdom Come!* Wm. B. Eerdmans Publishing Company, 1974.

Preisker, H., and Würthwein, E., *"Misthos,* etc.," in Gerhard Kittel (ed.), *Theological Dictionary of the New Testament,* Vol. IV, tr. by Geoffrey W. Bromiley. Wm. B. Eerdmans Publishing Company, 1967. Pp. 695–728.

Rad, Gerhard von, "Sin and Atonement," and "The Righteousness of Yahweh and Israel," in *Old Testament Theology,* Vol. I, tr. by D. M. G. Stalker. Harper & Row, Publishers, Inc., 1962. Pp. 262–72, 370–83.

Sanders, James A., *Suffering as Divine Discipline.* Colgate-Rochester Divinity School, 1955.

Schwartzback, Raymond H., "A Biblical Study of the Word 'Vengeance'," *Interpretation,* Vol. VI (1952), pp. 451–457.

Towner, W. Sibley, "Retribution," *The Interpreter's Dictionary of the Bible—Supplementary Volume.* Abingdon Press, 1976.

Wilder, Amos N., *Eschatology and Ethics in the Teaching of Jesus.* 2d ed. Harper & Row, Publishers, Inc., 1950.

LEX TALIONIS, COVENANT,
DEUTERONOMIC THEOLOGY, PROPHETISM

Clements, Ronald E., *Prophecy and Covenant.* London: SCM Press, Ltd., 1965.

———, *Prophecy and Tradition.* John Knox Press, 1975.

Cohn, H. H., "Talion," *Encyclopaedia Judaica*, Vol. XV (1971), cols. 741–742.

Diamond, A. S., *Primitive Law Past and Present*. Longmans, Green & Company, 1971.

Eichrodt, Walther, "Sin and Forgiveness," *Theology of the Old Testament*, Vol. II, tr. by J. A. Baker. The Westminster Press, 1967. Pp. 380–495.

Gammie, John G., "The Theology of Retribution in the Book of Deuteronomy," *Catholic Biblical Quarterly*, Vol. XXXII (1970), pp. 1–12.

Gerstenberger, Erhard, "The Woe-Oracles of the Prophets," *Journal of Biblical Literature*, Vol. LXXXI (1962), pp. 249–263.

Hillers, Delbert R., *Covenant: The History of a Biblical Idea*. The Johns Hopkins Press, 1969.

Jackson, B. S., "The Problem of Exod. XXI 22–5 (Ius talionis)," *Vetus Testamentum*, Vol. XXIII (1973), pp. 273–304.

McCarthy, Dennis J., S.J., *Treaty and Covenant*. Rome: Pontifical Biblical Institute, 1963.

McKeating, Henry, "Development of the Law of Homicide in Ancient Israel," *Vetus Testamentum*, Vol. XXV (1975), pp. 46–68.

Mendenhall, George, *Law and Covenant in Israel and the Ancient Near East*. Pittsburgh: The Biblical Colloquium, 1955.

Nicholson, Ernest W., *Deuteronomy and Tradition*. Fortress Press, 1967.

Paul, S. M., *Studies in the Book of the Covenant in the Light of Cuneiform and Biblical Law*. Leiden: E. J. Brill, Publishers, 1970.

Pedersen, Johannes, "Maintenance of Justice," *Israel: Its Life and Culture*, Vols. I-II, tr. by A. Møller. London: Oxford University Press, 1926. Pp. 378–452.

THE APOCALYPTIC SETTING
OF RETRIBUTIONAL THOUGHT

Beardslee, William A., "New Testament Apocalyptic in Recent Interpretation," *Interpretation*, Vol. XXV (1971), pp. 419–435.

Boers, H. W., "Apocalyptic Eschatology in I Cor. 15," *Interpretation*, Vol. XXI (1967), pp. 50–65.

Bronson, D. R., "Paul and Apocalyptic Judaism," *Journal of Biblical Literature,* Vol. LXXXIII (1964), pp. 287–292.

Hanson, Paul D., "Old Testament Apocalyptic Reexamined," *Interpretation,* Vol. XXV (1971), pp. 454–479.

————, *The Dawn of Apocalyptic.* Fortress Press, 1975.

Käsemann, Ernst, "The Beginnings of Christian Theology" and "On the Topic of Primitive Christian Apocalyptic" in *New Testament Questions of Today.* Fortress Press, 1969. Pp. 82–107, 108–137. Also in Robert W. Funk, ed., *Journal for Theology and the Church 6: Apocalypticism.* Herder & Herder, Inc. 1969. Pp. 17–46, 99–133.

Minear, Paul S., *I Saw a New Earth.* Washington: Corpus Books, 1968.

————, *Christian Hope and the Second Coming.* The Westminster Press, 1954.

Mussner, Franz, *Christ and the End of the World,* tr. by Maria von Eroes. University of Notre Dame Press, 1965.

Plöger, Otto, *Theocracy and Eschatology,* tr. by S. Rudman. John Knox Press, 1968.

Rissi, Mathias, *Time and History: A Study on the Revelation.* John Knox Press, 1966.

————, "The Kerygma of the Revelation to John," *Interpretation,* Vol. XXII (1968), pp. 3–17.

————, *The Future of the World: An Exegetical Study of Revelation 19:11—22:15.* London: SCM Press, Ltd., 1972.

Robinson, John A.T., *Jesus and His Coming.* London: SCM Press, Ltd., 1957.

Towner, W. Sibley, "Retributional Theology in the Apocalyptic Setting," *Union Seminary Quarterly Review,* Vol. XXVI (1971), pp. 203–214.

IMMORTALITY AND RESURRECTION

Cullmann, Oscar, *Immortality of the Soul or Resurrection of the Dead?* London: The Epworth Press, 1958.

Frost, Stanley B., "The Memorial of the Childless Man (A Study in Hebrew Thought on Immortality)," *Interpretation,* Vol. XXVI (1972), pp. 437–450.

Hanhart, Karel, "Paul's Hope in the Face of Death," *Journal of Biblical Literature*, Vol. LXXXVIII (1969), pp. 445–457.

Lewis, H. D., *The Self and Immortality*. The Seabury Press, Inc., 1973.

Nickelsburg, George W., *Resurrection, Immortality, and Eternal Life in Intertestamental Judaism*. Harvard University Press, 1972.

Sawyer, John F. A., "Hebrew Words for the Resurrection of the Dead," *Vetus Testamentum*, Vol. XXIII (1973), pp. 218–234.

Stendahl, Krister, ed., *Immortality and Resurrection*. The Macmillan Company, 1965.

Strawson, William, *Jesus and Future Life*. The Westminster Press, 1959.

Vawter, Bruce M., "Intimations of Immortality and the Old Testament," *Journal of Biblical Literature*, Vol. XCI (1972), pp. 158–171.

REWARD AND PUNISHMENT.
THE LAST JUDGMENT. HEAVEN AND HELL

Brandon, S. G. F., *The Judgment of the Dead*. London: Weidenfeld & Nicolson, 1967.

Buis, Harry, *The Doctrine of Eternal Punishment*. Presbyterian and Reformed Publishing Company, 1957.

Cohn, H. H., "Divine Punishment," *Encyclopaedia Judaica*, Vol. VI (1971), cols. 120–122.

Collins, John J., "Apocalyptic Eschatology as the Transcendence of Death," *Catholic Biblical Quarterly*, Vol. XXXVI (1974), pp. 21–43.

Cunliffe-Jones, H., "God's Judgment of the Individual After Death," *London Quarterly and Holborn Review*, Vol. XXXV (1967), pp. 116–128.

Edwards, David L., *The Last Things Now*. London: SCM Press, Ltd., 1969.

Fox, S. J., *Hell in Jewish Literature*. Northbrook, Ill.: Whitehall Company, 1972.

Hanhart, Karel, *The Intermediate State in the New Testament*. Franeker, The Netherlands: T. Wever, 1967.

Martin, James P., *The Last Judgment in Protestant Theology from Orthodoxy to Ritschl.* Wm. B. Eerdmans Publishing Company, 1963.

Melinek, A., "The Doctrine of Reward and Punishment in Biblical and Early Rabbinic Literature," in H. J. Zimmels, *et al.*, *Essays Presented to Chief Rabbi Israel Brodie. . . .* London: Soncino Press, 1967. Pp. 275–290.

Morris, Leon, *The Biblical Doctrine of Judgment.* London: Tyndale Press, 1960.

Motyer, J. A., *After Death: A Sure and Certain Hope?* The Westminster Press, 1966.

Pusey, E. B., *What Is of Faith as to Everlasting Punishment?* Oxford: James Parker, 1880.

Rabinowitz, Louis I., *et al.*, "Reward and Punishment," in *Encyclopaedia Judaica*, Vol. XIV (1971), cols. 134–139.

Rowell, Geoffrey, *Hell and the Victorians.* Oxford University Press, 1974.

Ru, G. de, "The Conception of Reward in the Teaching of Jesus," *Novum Testamentum*, Vol. VIII (1966), pp. 202–222.

Ryder-Smith, C., *The Bible Doctrine of the Hereafter.* London: The Epworth Press, 1958.

Tromp, N. J., *Primitive Conceptions of Death and the Nether World in the Old Testament.* Rome: Pontifical Biblical Institute, 1969.

Walker, D. P., *The Decline of Hell: Seventeenth-Century Discussions of Eternal Punishment.* The University of Chicago Press, 1964.

THE PLACE OF RETRIBUTION
IN SYSTEMATIC THEOLOGY

Altizer, Thomas J. J., "The Dialectic of Ancient and Modern Apocalypticism," *Journal of the American Academy of Religion*, Vol. XXXIX (1971), pp. 312–320.

Baxter, Richard, *The Saints' Everlasting Rest* (1650), ed. by J. T. Wilkinson. London: The Epworth Press, 1962.

Berkouwer, G. C., *The Triumph of Grace in the Theology of Karl Barth*, tr. by Harry R. Boer. Wm. B. Eerdmans Publishing Company, 1956.

Braaten, Carl E., "The Significance of Apocalypticism for System-atic Theology," *Interpretation,* Vol. XXV (1971), pp. 480–499.

Brunner, Emil, *Eternal Hope,* tr. by Harold Knight. The Westmin-ster Press, 1954.

Kuiper, R. B., *For Whom Did Christ Die?* Wm. B. Eerdmans Pub-lishing Company, 1959.

Leith, John H., *Creeds of the Churches.* Rev. ed. John Knox Press, 1973.

Pittenger, Norman, *"The Last Things" in a Process Perspective.* London: The Epworth Press, 1970.

The Presbyterian Church in the United States, "A Study of Univer-salism," received by the 114th General Assembly. Atlanta: Office of the General Assembly, 1974.

Quistorp, H., *Calvin's Doctrine of the Last Things,* tr. by Harold Knight. John Knox Press, 1955.

Schechter, Solomon, "Divine Retribution in Rabbinic Literature," reprinted in A. Corré, ed., *Understanding the Talmud.* New York: KTAV, 1975. Pp. 381–393.

Sontag, Frederick, *The God of Evil: An Argument from the Exis-tence of the Devil.* Harper & Row, Publishers, Inc., 1970.

_____, *God, Why Did You Do That?* The Westminster Press, 1970.

Stuermann, W. E., *The Divine Destroyer: A Theology of Good and Evil.* The Westminster Press, 1967.

INDEX OF
SCRIPTURAL CITATIONS

In some cases a number of short passages have been indexed together under an inclusive reference. To find mention of a specific verse or passage, refer to all the pages listed in an entry. All references are to the English text.